I0625394

CONSCIOUSNESS

THE POWER OF VIBRATION AND FREQUENCY

N. J. POWELL

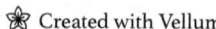

CONSCIOUSNESS: THE POWER OF VIBRATION AND FREQUENCY

Embark on a captivating journey into the depths of consciousness with "Consciousness: The Power of Vibration and Frequency." Explore the profound interplay between consciousness and subtle energies, from ancient traditional wisdom to modern science. Uncover how vibration and frequency transform the human experience, unlocking new dimensions of awareness and spiritual growth. Delve into their impact on the energy body and consciousness, from environmental forces to investigating the metaphysical realm where ancient beliefs intersect with modern practices. Explore the mysteries of spiritual and dream states, guided by illuminating research and practical wisdom. This comprehensive study offers valuable insights and actionable guidance for personal evolution, while providing clarity and simplicity for all readers.

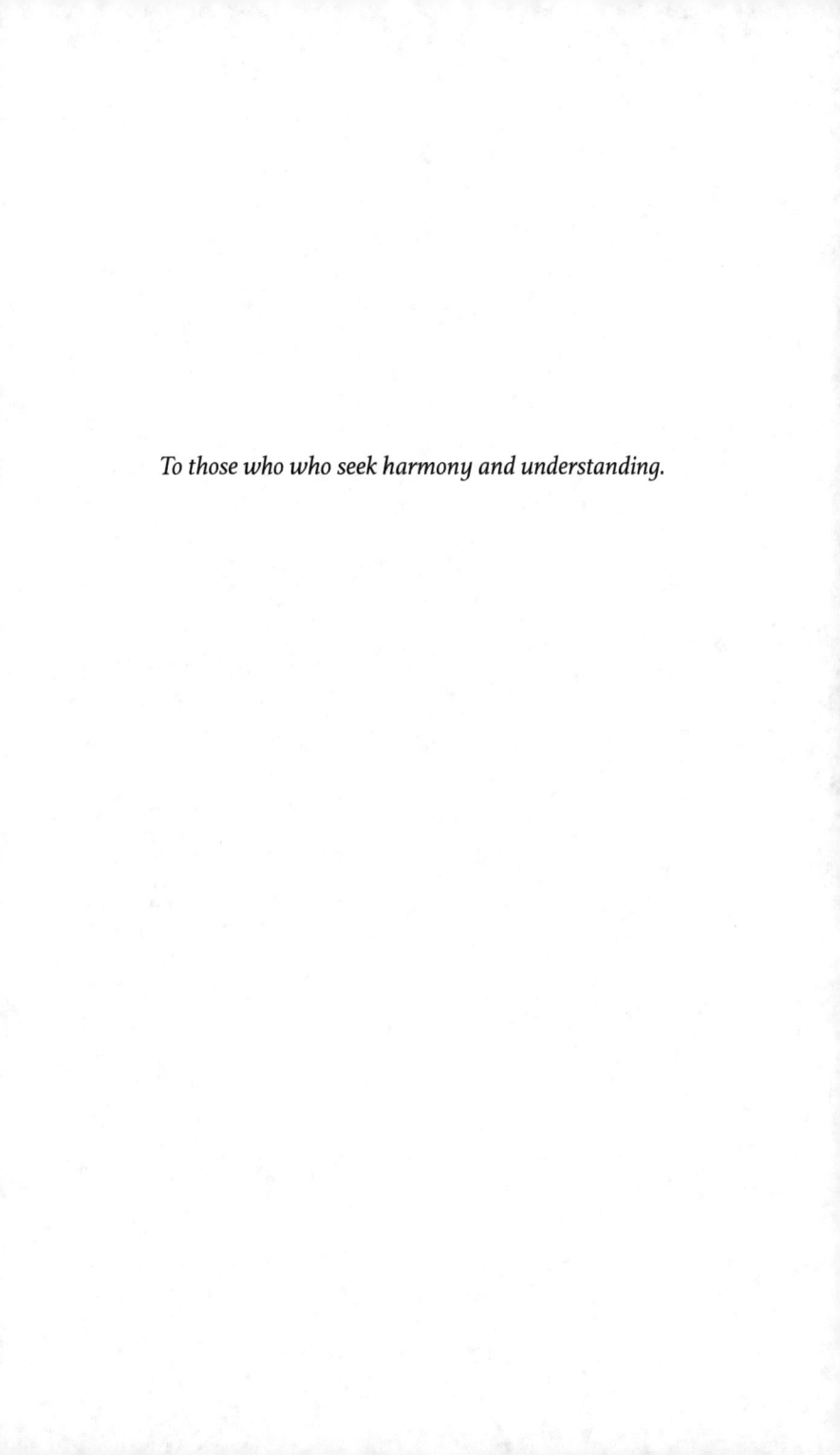

To those who who seek harmony and understanding.

"Within the boundless expanse of consciousness lies the infinite tapestry of possibilities, waiting to be explored, understood, and woven into the fabric of our collective evolution." Unknown

CONTENTS

FOREWORD

Welcome to a journey of exploration into the depths of consciousness—a realm where physical reality blurs, and existence unfolds across infinite dimensions. Within these pages, we embark on a quest to unravel the mysteries of consciousness and shed light on the profound influence of energy, vibration, and frequency on our innermost being.

At the core of our exploration lies the fundamental understanding that consciousness transcends mere cognition. It forms a vast, interconnected web that permeates the fabric of existence. It binds us to the universe, animates our being, and serves as a gateway to profound insight and understanding.

Throughout history, sages, scholars, and seekers alike have pondered the nature of consciousness, seeking to unlock its mysteries and tap into its boundless potential. In my quest for understanding, I have explored the realms of spirituality, philosophy, science, and mysticism, each offering its own unique perspective on the nature of reality and the human experience.

In this book, we delve into the profound interplay between consciousness and the subtle energies that shape our perception of the world. We explore energy as the currency of existence, the vibrations resonating within and around us, and the frequencies that weave the tapestry of our reality.

Drawing from ancient Eastern wisdom to the cutting-edge insights of modern science, we illuminate the dance of energy, vibration, and frequency within human experience. We examine how these subtle forces influence our thoughts, emotions, and perceptions, shaping the very fabric of our reality.

As we journey into the depths of consciousness, we uncover the transformative power of energy, vibration, and frequency, and their profound impact on our spiritual, emotional, and physical well-being. We discover how harmonising these forces can lead to greater clarity, insight, and awakening, while discordant vibrations may manifest as dissonance, imbalance, and disconnection from our true selves.

Ultimately, this book invites you to embark on a journey of self-discovery and transformation—a testament to the boundless potential of the human spirit and the infinite possibilities that aligning with consciousness's higher frequencies offer.

May these pages serve as a guiding light on your path, illuminating your exploration of consciousness's depths and embracing the transformative power of energy, vibration, and frequency.

With deepest reverence for the mysteries ahead.

INTRODUCTION

Exploring the Depths of Consciousness: The Power of Frequency, Vibrations and Energy

In the vast tapestry of human experience, consciousness stands as an enigmatic realm, teeming with untold possibilities and mysteries awaiting revelation. Envision yourself at the threshold of this realm, where the boundaries of physical reality dissolve, and the essence of existence unfolds across a myriad of dimensions. Within this mystical landscape, we embark on a transformative journey—a journey delving deep into the profound interplay between consciousness, frequency, vibrations, and energy.

Imagine a world where thoughts dance to the rhythm of energy, where emotions resonate with the vibrations of the universe, and where life pulsates with vitality. This is the world we are about to explore—a realm of boundless potential and infinite wonder.

In the pages ahead, we unravel the intricate tapestry of consciousness, probing its depths and uncovering the limitless potential it holds for personal growth, conscious evolution, and collective transformation. Drawing upon insights from neuroscience, quantum physics, psychology, and ancient traditional wisdom, we embark on a multidimensional odyssey transcending the boundaries of conventional understanding.

At the heart of our exploration lies the Energy Body—an intricate matrix of subtle energies permeating and interconnecting every aspect of our being. Bridging the physical and metaphysical realms, the Energy Body serves as a conduit for healing, transformation, and conscious awakening. From the timeless wisdom of Eastern traditions to the cutting-edge insights of modern energy medicine, we reveal the profound significance of the Energy Body in facilitating holistic well-being.

Furthermore, through an exploration of vibrations and frequencies—the language of creation—we delve into vibrational medicine, sound therapy, and the transformative power of resonance, shedding light on their profound influence on consciousness and overall well-being. Through mindfulness practices, meditation techniques, and the cultivation of inner wisdom, we unlock doorways to expanded awareness and conscious evolution.

Welcome to the exploration of consciousness—an adventure of discovery and illumination with limitless horizons. Join us as we embark on this sacred quest, journeying together through the depths of consciousness and embracing the radiant essence of our true nature.

1

HUMAN CONSCIOUSNESS

Unraveling the Meaning of Consciousness

Consciousness, the very essence of human existence, remains one of the most profound and enduring mysteries of our time. In this chapter, we embark on a journey to unravel the multifaceted layers of consciousness, exploring its diverse manifestations, philosophical implications, and scientific underpinnings.

THE ESSENCE of Consciousness

The essence of consciousness lies in our awareness of being - our subjective experience of thoughts, emotions, sensations, and perceptions that shape our reality (Chalmers, 1995). It's like an ineffable spark of awareness lighting up our inner world and guiding our interactions with the external environment.

. . .

AS WE EXPLORE CONSCIOUSNESS, we venture into the depths of subjectivity, where the very core of our existence reveals itself through intricate layers of thought, emotion, and perception.

CONSCIOUSNESS GOES BEYOND EMPIRICAL OBSERVATION; it dwells in the realm of subjective experience and introspection (Nagel, 1974). It serves as the seat of our deepest thoughts, desires, and aspirations—an inner sanctum where the complexity and nuance of our existence unfold.

THE PHILOSOPHICAL IMPLICATIONS of Consciousness

Throughout human history, philosophers, theologians, and mystics have wrestled with the mysterious nature of consciousness, contemplating its origins, essence, and significance (Descartes, 1641). From the Cartesian duality of mind and body to Eastern notions of non-duality and interconnectedness, a variety of philosophical frameworks offer unique perspectives on consciousness.

THE SCIENTIFIC QUEST for Understanding

In the realm of science, consciousness poses a formidable challenge—a conundrum that resists easy explanation or reduction (Dennett, 1991). Neuroscientists, cognitive psychologists, and physicists all strive to unravel the neural correlates of consciousness, investigating the complexities of brain function and neural networks in pursuit of the elusive "hard problem" (Chalmers, 1995).

. . .

WHILE NUMEROUS THEORIES and models have been proposed, there hasn't been a definitive breakthrough providing a comprehensive explanation of consciousness. However, significant advancements have occurred in the field. Some notable areas of progress include:

NEUROSCIENCE: Scientists have made significant strides in identifying brain regions and neural correlates associated with consciousness. Techniques such as functional magnetic resonance imaging (fMRI) and electroencephalography (EEG) have enabled researchers to observe brain activity and its relation to conscious experiences. Studies on patients with brain injuries, including those in vegetative states, have offered insights into the neural mechanisms underlying consciousness (Boly et al., 2008; Laureys et al., 2000).

FREQUENCY TUNING: Research has shed light on how neurons respond to different frequencies of sensory input from the surrounding environment. Neurons exhibit distinct patterns of activity in response to various frequencies, with some being more sensitive to high-frequency stimuli and others to lower frequencies. This phenomenon, known as frequency tuning, plays a crucial role in information processing and perception within the brain.

INTEGRATED INFORMATION THEORY (IIT): Proposed by neuroscientist Giulio Tononi, IIT posits that consciousness arises from the integration of information in the brain. It suggests that the more integrated and irreducible the information is, the higher the level of consciousness. While still debated,

IIT provides a framework for quantifying and studying consciousness (Tononi, 2004).

GLOBAL WORKSPACE THEORY: Developed by cognitive scientist Bernard Baars, the Global Workspace Theory proposes that consciousness emerges from the global integration of information in the brain. According to this theory, certain brain areas act as a "global workspace" where information is broadcasted and becomes accessible to other cognitive processes (Baars, 1988).

PSYCHEDELIC RESEARCH: Recent studies on psychedelic substances like psilocybin and LSD have revived interest in altered states of consciousness. Research suggests that these substances may induce profound changes in consciousness by disrupting normal brain activity and promoting neural connectivity (Carhart-Harris et al., 2014; Lebedev et al., 2015).

ARTIFICIAL INTELLIGENCE: Advances in artificial intelligence and machine learning have led to the development of computational models of consciousness. Researchers aim to simulate conscious experiences in machines and use artificial systems as tools for understanding consciousness (Chalmers, 1995). While researchers explore various approaches and theories, simulating conscious experiences in machines is still in its infancy.

DESPITE THESE BREAKTHROUGHS, the nature of consciousness remains a complex and multifaceted phenomenon that continues to challenge our understanding.

· · ·

Conclusion - Embracing the Mystery

In the vast expanse of human inquiry, consciousness stands as a testament to the enduring mysteries of existence—a riddle wrapped in an enigma, waiting to be unraveled (Searle, 1992). As we journey deeper into the labyrinth of consciousness, may we approach the mystery with humility, curiosity, and wonder, embracing the boundless possibilities that lie beyond the veil of perception.

In our exploration of consciousness, let's embrace its mysteries with awe and reverence, recognising that understanding is not only a journey of self-discovery but an exploration of the cosmos.

Advancements in Human Consciousness Through Evolution and Generations

Human consciousness, the awareness of one's existence and surroundings, has undergone significant advancements throughout evolutionary history and across generations. This chapter explores the evolution of human consciousness, highlighting key milestones, contributing factors, and the implications for individual and collective experience.

EVOLUTIONARY PERSPECTIVES: From an evolutionary standpoint, the development of human consciousness can be traced back millions of years to our early hominid ancestors. The emergence of complex cognitive abilities, including self-awareness, symbolic thought, and social cognition, marked significant milestones in the evolution of human consciousness (Deacon, 1997).

THE EVOLUTION of the human brain, particularly the expansion of the neocortex, enabled higher-order thinking, language acquisition, and problem-solving abilities that distinguished early humans from other species (Dunbar, 1998).

CULTURAL AND TECHNOLOGICAL INNOVATIONS: Throughout human history, cultural and technological innovations have been instrumental in shaping the trajectory of human consciousness. The development of agriculture, writing systems, and organised religion marked key transitions in human cultural evolution, fostering new forms of social organisation, communication, and symbolic expression (Diamond, 1997).

·   ·   ·

TECHNOLOGICAL ADVANCEMENTS, from the invention of the wheel to the internet age, have expanded the scope of human knowledge, connectivity, and creativity, catalysing shifts in consciousness and collective awareness (Harari, 2014).

PSYCHOLOGICAL AND PHILOSOPHICAL PERSPECTIVES: Psychological and philosophical perspectives offer profound insights into the nature and dynamics of human consciousness. From Freud's psychoanalytic theory to Jung's concept of the collective unconscious, scholars have explored the depths of human psyche and the interplay between conscious and unconscious processes (Freud, 1915; Jung, 1933).

EXISTENTIALIST PHILOSOPHERS such as Sartre and Camus delved into questions of individual freedom, responsibility, and the search for meaning in a seemingly indifferent universe, challenging conventional notions of self and reality (Sartre, 1943; Camus, 1942).

SPIRITUAL AND TRANSPERSONAL DIMENSIONS: Spiritual and transpersonal dimensions of consciousness offer alternative frameworks for understanding human existence and experience. From ancient wisdom traditions to modern spiritual movements, individuals have explored states of consciousness beyond the confines of the ego, seeking union with the divine, transcendence of suffering, and realisation of higher truths (Wilber, 1996).

. . .

PRACTICES SUCH AS MEDITATION, yoga, and psychedelics have been used for millennia to induce altered states of consciousness and facilitate spiritual awakening, leading to profound insights into the nature of reality and the human condition (Grof, 2000).

NEUROSCIENTIFIC INSIGHTS: Advances in neuroscience have shed light on the neural correlates of consciousness, unraveling the complex interplay of brain regions and neural networks underlying subjective experience and self-awareness (Koch, 2004).

NEUROIMAGING techniques such as functional magnetic resonance imaging (fMRI) and electroencephalography (EEG) have provided unprecedented insights into the neural basis of perception, cognition, and consciousness (Tononi & Koch, 2008).

THE STUDY OF NEUROPLASTICITY, the brain's capacity to reorganise and adapt in response to experience, suggests that consciousness is not fixed but dynamic, shaped by environmental influences, social interactions, and cognitive practices (Doidge, 2007).

CONCLUSION

The advancements in human consciousness through evolution and generations reflect the dynamic interplay of biological, cultural, psychological, and spiritual factors. By exploring the complex tapestry of human consciousness, we gain deeper insights into the nature of existence, the mysteries of the mind, and the potential for individual and collective transformation.

Beyond the Individual: Collective Consciousness and Cultural Perspectives

Consciousness extends beyond the boundaries of individual experience, permeating the collective psyche and cultural zeit-geist (Jung, 1953). From the shared myths and symbols of ancient civilisations to the emergent phenomena of social movements and cultural revolutions, collective consciousness shapes the tapestry of human history and evolution.

Advancement in Collective Consciousness Through Generations

The concept of collective consciousness refers to the shared beliefs, values, and perceptions that shape the worldview and behaviour of a society or group. Across generations, humanity has witnessed an evolution in collective consciousness marked by shifts in cultural, social, and philosophical paradigms.

UNDERSTANDING the advancement in collective consciousness through the generations offers insights into the progress, challenges, and transformative potential of human civilisation.

CULTURAL AND SOCIETAL SHIFTS: Throughout history, societies have undergone profound transformations in collective consciousness driven by cultural, technological, and ideological developments. From the agrarian societies of ancient civilisations to the industrialised nations of the modern era, each generation has contributed to the evolution of collective consciousness through its unique experiences, innovations, and challenges (Toynbee, 1946).

. . .

CULTURAL MOVEMENTS such as the Renaissance, Enlightenment, and Industrial Revolution have played pivotal roles in shaping collective consciousness, catalysing shifts in worldview, values, and social structures (Eisenstein, 2011).

TECHNOLOGICAL ADVANCEMENTS: The advent of technology, particularly in the digital age, has accelerated the exchange of ideas, information, and perspectives, fostering a more interconnected and globalised collective consciousness. The internet, social media, and telecommunications have facilitated communication and collaboration across geographical and cultural boundaries, enabling the emergence of global movements, social activism, and cultural exchange (Castells, 1996).

TECHNOLOGICAL INNOVATIONS HAVE ALSO RAISED ethical and existential questions about the impact of artificial intelligence, biotechnology, and virtual reality on collective consciousness and human identity (Harari, 2016).

SOCIAL AND ENVIRONMENTAL AWARENESS: In recent decades, there has been a growing awareness and concern about pressing social and environmental issues, including climate change, social inequality, and human rights. This heightened consciousness has led to grassroots movements, advocacy campaigns, and policy initiatives aimed at addressing systemic injustices and promoting sustainability, equity, and social justice (Klein, 2014).

. . .

THE RISE OF ENVIRONMENTALISM, feminism, civil rights, and other social movements reflects a collective awakening to the interconnectedness of humanity and the need for collective action and solidarity (Hawken, 2007).

SPIRITUAL AND PHILOSOPHICAL AWAKENING: Alongside material progress, there has been a resurgence of interest in spirituality, mysticism, and holistic wellness as people seek deeper meaning, purpose, and connection in their lives. This spiritual awakening transcends religious dogma and institutionalised belief systems, encompassing diverse spiritual practices, mindfulness techniques, and philosophical inquiry (Tolle, 1997).

THE INTEGRATION of Eastern and Western spiritual traditions, as well as the exploration of consciousness-expanding practices such as meditation, yoga, and psychedelics, reflects a collective shift towards greater self-awareness, compassion, and inner transformation (Pollan, 2018).

INTERGENERATIONAL DIALOGUE AND WISDOM TRANSMISSION: Intergenerational dialogue and wisdom transmission play a crucial role in advancing collective consciousness, as older generations impart knowledge, values, and insights to younger generations, while younger generations challenge established norms, question authority, and catalyse innovation and change (Mannheim, 1928).

THE EXCHANGE OF IDEAS, experiences, and perspectives across generations fosters a dynamic and adaptive collective consciousness that evolves in response to changing social, cultural, and environmental dynamics.

Conclusion

The advancement in collective consciousness through the generations reflects the ongoing evolution of human society and civilisation. By embracing diversity, dialogue, and shared values, humanity can harness its collective wisdom and creativity to navigate the complexities of the modern world and build a more equitable, sustainable, and harmonious future.

The Rise of the 'Woke Generation'

The term "woke generation" has gained prominence in contemporary discourse, referring to a demographic of individuals who are socially and politically conscious, aware, and actively engaged in issues related to social justice, equity, and systemic change. This chapter explores the concept of the "woke generation," its origins, implications, and impact on society.

ORIGINS AND EVOLUTION: THE TERM "WOKE" originated in African American Vernacular English (AAVE) and has historical roots in the civil rights movement of the 1960s, where it was used to describe individuals who were awake and aware of racial injustice and oppression (Eberhardt, 2019). Over time, the term has evolved to encompass broader issues of social justice, including gender equality, LGBTQ+ rights, environmental justice, and economic equity.

THE RISE OF THE "WOKE GENERATION" is often attributed to the proliferation of social media, digital activism, and increased access to information and diverse perspectives. Platforms such as Twitter, Instagram, and TikTok have become powerful tools for organising, mobilising, and raising awareness about social and political issues on a global scale (Brock, 2018).

CHARACTERISTICS AND VALUES: Members of the "woke generation" prioritise social justice, inclusivity, and diversity, advocating empathy, intersectionality, and allyship (DiAngelo, 2018).

. . .

THEIR VALUES ARE REFLECTED in language, cultural expressions, and activism, addressing concepts like cultural appropriation and privilege (Khan-Cullors & Bandele, 2017).

CRITIQUES AND CHALLENGES: While instrumental in social justice discussions, the "woke generation" faces criticism for performative activism and ideological polarisation (Hess, 2017; Lukianoff & Haidt, 2018).

IMPACT AND INFLUENCE: THE "WOKE GENERATION" has influenced mainstream culture, politics, and institutions, driving movements like Black Lives Matter and climate activism (Crenshaw, 2017). Its impact is seen in corporate policies, media representation, and educational curricula (Klein, 2019).

FUTURE DIRECTIONS: The trajectory of the "woke generation" remains uncertain as it adapts to changing landscapes, with ongoing debates reflecting broader conversations about identity and social change (Kendi, 2019; Kumar, 2018).

CONCLUSION

The "woke generation" represents a powerful force for social transformation and systemic change, challenging norms, confronting injustice, and striving for a more inclusive and equitable society. While critiques and challenges abound, the enduring commitment of the "woke" movement to justice, solidarity, and collective action holds promise for a more just and equitable future.

Higher Consciousness and Ascended Consciousness

Higher consciousness and ascended consciousness represent elevated states of awareness and spiritual evolution that transcend ordinary perception and egoic identity. Emerging research in neuroscience and consciousness studies offers valuable insights into the neural correlates and transformative effects of higher states of consciousness.

UNDERSTANDING HIGHER CONSCIOUSNESS: Higher consciousness refers to expanded states of awareness characterised by heightened perception, insight, and interconnectedness with the cosmos. Individuals experiencing higher states of consciousness may feel profound states of peace, bliss, and unity with all existence. These states often involve a deep sense of presence, transcendence of egoic identification, and connection to the universal source of consciousness.

NEURAL CORRELATES OF HIGHER CONSCIOUSNESS: Neuroscientific research suggests that higher states of consciousness are associated with unique patterns of brain activity and neural connectivity. Studies using neuroimaging techniques such as fMRI and EEG have identified changes in brain regions involved in attention, self-awareness, and emotion regulation during meditation, contemplative practices, and psychedelic experiences (Brewer et al., 2011; Lutz et al., 2007).

BRAIN REGIONS such as the prefrontal cortex, insula, and default mode network (DMN) have been implicated in the modulation of consciousness and the integration of diverse aspects of experience. Shifts in activity and connectivity within these regions may underlie the transformational effects of higher states of consciousness on perception, cognition, and behaviour (Carhart-Harris et al., 2014).

Ascended Consciousness and Spiritual Evolution: Ascended consciousness represents the pinnacle of spiritual evolution, where individuals transcend the limitations of egoic identity and embody higher qualities of love, wisdom, and compassion. In ascended states of consciousness, individuals may experience direct communion with the divine, access to universal wisdom, and alignment with the highest potentials of human existence.

While empirical research on ascended consciousness is limited, anecdotal reports and spiritual traditions suggest that profound shifts in perception and behaviour accompany the realisation of ascended states of consciousness. Individuals may undergo profound transformations in their worldview, values, and relationships, leading to greater harmony, altruism, and service to humanity (Wilber, 2000).

Integration of Science and Spirituality: The study of higher consciousness and ascended consciousness bridges the gap between science and spirituality, offering a holistic under-standing of the nature of reality and human potential. Inte-grating insights from neuroscience, psychology, and spiritual traditions enables a more comprehensive exploration of consciousness and its transformative effects on individual and collective well-being.

. . .

Conclusion

Exploring higher consciousness and ascended consciousness provides valuable insights into the nature of human consciousness and its potential for spiritual evolution. By integrating findings from brain studies and spiritual wisdom, we can deepen our understanding of consciousness and cultivate states of awareness that promote healing, growth, and awakening.

2

UNDERSTANDING VIBRATIONS AND FREQUENCY

The Fundamentals of Vibrations and Frequencies

Vibrations and frequencies, often regarded as the language of creation, form the very essence of the universe, intricately weaving the fabric of reality and exerting a profound influence on human consciousness. In this chapter, we embark on a journey to unravel the complexities of vibrations and frequencies, delving into their profound significance, mechanisms, and implications for the human experience.

DEFINITION AND EXPLANATION

Vibrations refer to the oscillations or movements of particles or energy waves, characterised by their amplitude, frequency, and wavelength (Rosen, 2019). Frequencies, on the other hand, denote the number of oscillations per unit of time, measured in hertz (Hz). Together, vibrations and frequencies form the basis of all energy and matter, from subatomic particles to galaxies.

. . .

The Human Energy System

In the context of human consciousness, vibrations and frequencies play a central role in shaping the human energy system, which encompasses the physical body, emotions, thoughts, and spirit (McTaggart, 2002). Each aspect of the human energy system emits its own unique vibrational frequency, contributing to the overall vibrational signature of an individual.

The Dynamic Interplay of Vibrations and Consciousness

Emotional Resonance: Emotions are energetic expressions that resonate at specific frequencies, influencing our mood, behaviour, and perception of reality (Goleman, 1995). Positive emotions, such as love and gratitude, vibrate at higher frequencies, while negative emotions, such as fear and anger, resonate at lower frequencies.

Thought Patterns: Thoughts are energetic currents that generate vibrational frequencies based on their content and intensity (Dispenza, 2012). Positive thoughts and beliefs elevate our vibrational frequency, expanding our consciousness and enhancing our ability to manifest desired outcomes.

Spiritual Awakening: Spiritual awakening involves a shift in consciousness towards higher levels of awareness and enlightenment (Tolle, 2004). This transformative process often entails a raising of vibrational frequency, allowing individuals to transcend egoic limitations and perceive the interconnectedness of all life.

. . .

HARNESSING Vibrations for Healing and Transformation

Sound Therapy: Sound has the power to entrain brainwave patterns, induce relaxation, and promote healing on physical, emotional, and spiritual levels (Gassmann et al., 2013). Practices such as chanting, singing bowls, and binaural beats leverage the therapeutic potential of sound vibrations to restore balance and harmony to the body and mind.

Mindfulness and Meditation: Mindfulness and meditation practices facilitate a deepening of awareness and attunement to the present moment (Kabat-Zinn, 1990). By quieting the mind and tuning into the subtle vibrations of consciousness, individuals can access inner peace, clarity, and insight.

READERS interested in exploring the therapeutic potential of vibrations and frequencies in healing and transformation are encouraged to delve deeper into Chapter 7: Healing and Well-being.

CONCLUSION

Vibrations and frequencies serve as the language of the universe, guiding the evolution of consciousness and the interconnectedness of all life. By understanding and harnessing the power of vibrations, we can cultivate greater harmony, balance, and well-being in ourselves and the world around us.

Vibrations and Frequency in the Human Body

The human body is not merely a physical entity but a complex system of energy, vibrations, and frequencies that interact to maintain balance and harmony. From the cellular level to the organs and systems, every aspect of our physiology resonates with its unique vibrational frequency, contributing to the dynamic equilibrium that sustains life.

CELLULAR VIBRATIONS: At the foundation of human existence lies the cellular realm, where trillions of cells pulsate with vitality and energy. Each cell emits its own vibrational frequency, influenced by its composition, function, and surrounding environment (Rubik, 2002). From the rhythmic beating of the heart cells to the synchronised firing of neurons in the brain, cellular vibrations orchestrate the symphony of life within the human body.

BIOENERGETIC FIELDS: Surrounding and permeating the physical body is a subtle matrix of bioenergetic fields, often referred to as the aura or energy field. These fields extend beyond the physical boundaries and serve as the interface between the body and the external environment (Gerber, 2001). Through techniques such as biofield therapies and energy medicine, practitioners seek to assess and manipulate these fields to promote health and well-being.

CHAKRAS AND ENERGY CENTRES: Central to many spiritual and healing traditions are the chakras, or energy centres, which serve as focal points for the flow of vital energy throughout the body (Judith, 2004). Each chakra corresponds to specific organs, emotions, and aspects of consciousness, vibrating at distinct frequencies that influence physical, emotional, and spiritual health. Practices such as yoga, meditation, and energy healing aim to balance and harmonise these chakras, restoring equilibrium to the energetic system.

FREQUENCY MEDICINE: Emerging research in the field of frequency medicine explores the therapeutic potential of sound, light, and electromagnetic frequencies in promoting health and healing (Rinaldi et al., 2020). Technologies such as bioresonance therapy and frequency-specific micro-currents target specific frequencies associated with physiological imbalances, aiming to restore coherence and function to the body's energetic pathways.

RESONANCE AND HARMONY: At the core of vibrational medicine lies the principle of resonance—the phenomenon in which two objects vibrating at similar frequencies synchronise and amplify each other's energy (Oschman, 2000). By exposing the body to resonant frequencies through music, sound therapy, or vibrational remedies, practitioners seek to entrain the body's vibrations toward states of balance, coherence, and optimal functioning.

CONCLUSION

The human body is a dynamic tapestry of vibrations and frequencies intricately woven into the fabric of existence. From the cellular level to the subtle realms of consciousness, these vibrational patterns significantly influence our physical, emotional, and spiritual well-being. By comprehending and harnessing the power of vibrations and frequency, we embark on a profound journey of self-discovery, healing, and transformation, ultimately leading to a harmonious and balanced state of being.

Exploring the Dynamic Interplay of Vibrations and Frequency in Human Health and Well-being

Vibrations and frequency can significantly impact the human body on various levels, from physiological to psychological. Research suggests that exposure to certain frequencies and vibrations can influence mood, cognition, and even physical health. For instance, studies indicate that low-frequency vibrations may affect the musculoskeletal system, potentially leading to discomfort or injury over time (Alam, 2016). Moreover, specific frequencies, such as those found in music or sound therapy, have been shown to induce relaxation, reduce stress, and promote healing (Thoma et al., 2017). Understanding the effects of vibrations and frequency on the human body is crucial for promoting overall well-being and health.

Cosmic Vibration, Frequencies, and Electromagnetic Waves: Exploring the Fabric of the Universe

The concept of cosmic vibration represents an ancient and profound understanding that the universe is in a constant state of motion and resonance. In this chapter, we delve into the idea of cosmic vibration, examining its origins, implications, and transformative effects on the cosmos.

THE PRIMORDIAL PULSE OF CREATION: According to various spiritual and philosophical traditions, cosmic vibration is believed to be the primordial pulse of creation, the source from which all existence emanates. In Hindu cosmology, the concept of Nada Brahman suggests that the universe is a manifestation of sound vibrations, echoing the divine resonance of the cosmic Aum (Goswami, 1995). The ancient Greek notion of the "Music of the Spheres" posits that celestial bodies, including planets and stars, emit harmonious vibrations that resonate with the cosmic symphony, reflecting the underlying order and beauty of the cosmos (Burkert, 1985).

HARMONY AND DISSONANCE in the Cosmic Orchestra: Cosmic vibration encompasses a spectrum of frequencies and harmonics that permeate the fabric of the universe, shaping its structure, dynamics, and evolution. From the subatomic realm to the cosmic scale, vibrations manifest as waves of energy, influencing the behaviour of particles, galaxies, and cosmic phenomena (Halpern, 2012). The balance between harmony and dissonance in the cosmic orchestra is reflected in the dynamic interplay of cosmic forces, such as gravity, electromagnetism, and the weak and strong nuclear forces. The cosmic dance of creation and destruction unfolds in accordance with the rhythmic cycles of expansion and contraction, birth and dissolution (Hawking, 1988).

THE UNIFIED FIELD OF CONSCIOUSNESS: In contemporary physics, the concept of cosmic vibration finds resonance with the notion of a unified field of consciousness, a fundamental matrix of existence that underlies all phenomena and experiences. The unified field theory seeks to reconcile the disparate realms of quantum mechanics and relativity, elucidating the interconnectedness of matter, energy, and consciousness

(Hagelin, 1994). Proponents of the unified field theory propose that cosmic vibration is the substrate of reality, the medium through which consciousness interacts with the material world. The vibrational nature of existence suggests that consciousness itself is a fundamental aspect of the cosmic symphony, imbuing the universe with meaning, purpose, and intelligence (Talbot, 1991).

THE DANCE OF COSMIC EVOLUTION: Cosmic vibration plays a pivotal role in the evolutionary dynamics of the universe, driving the emergence of complexity, diversity, and order. From the formation of galaxies and stars to the evolution of life on Earth, vibrational frequencies orchestrate the unfolding of cosmic evolution, guiding the trajectory of cosmic history (Sagan, 1980). The evolutionary journey of the cosmos is characterised by moments of synergy and coherence, as well as periods of chaos and disruption. Cosmic vibrations sculpt the cosmic landscape, shaping the emergence of galaxies, stars, planets, and life forms, and imbuing the universe with beauty, wonder, and mystery (Gleiser, 2019).

HUMAN CONSCIOUSNESS AND COSMIC HARMONY: As sentient beings endowed with consciousness, humans are attuned to the cosmic symphony, resonating with the vibrational frequencies of the universe. Through practices such as meditation, contemplation, and mindfulness, individuals can attune themselves to the subtle rhythms and harmonies of cosmic vibration, cultivating a deeper sense of connection and resonance with the cosmos (Hameroff & Penrose, 1996). The exploration of cosmic vibration invites individuals to embark on a journey of self-discovery and spiritual awakening, awakening to the intrinsic unity and interdependence of all existence. By aligning with the cosmic pulse of creation, humans can participate in the co-creation of a harmonious and compassionate world, embodying the timeless wisdom of cosmic consciousness (Capra, 1975).

CONCLUSION

Cosmic vibration is a fundamental aspect of the universe, shaping its structure, dynamics, and evolution. From the subatomic realm to the cosmic scale, vibrations permeate the fabric of existence, inviting sentient beings to participate in the cosmic dance of creation and transformation.

3

METAPHYSICAL AND CULTURAL PERSPECTIVES

Now we delve beyond the confines of the physical body to explore the dynamic realm of energy that constitutes our being, the metaphysical body. Here, we embark on a journey through a tapestry of cultural beliefs surrounding the energy body, including Japanese perspectives on Ki (Chi) and ancient Greek insights into Pneuma. We also dissect the significance of meridians in Traditional Chinese Medicine and unravel the intricacies of the Ayurvedic energetic body. As we navigate these cultural and philosophical landscapes, we encounter the profound dimensions of consciousness through the prism of Kundalini, and spiritual energy and vitality implicit in many Christian teachings. Ultimately, our exploration sheds light on the pivotal role of the energy body in shaping individual experiences and perceptions of reality.

The Metaphysical Body in Humans

The metaphysical body refers to aspects of human existence beyond the physical realm, encompassing energy fields, consciousness, and spiritual dimensions. Understanding the metaphysical body provides insights into the interconnectedness of mind, body, and spirit, as well as holistic approaches to health and well-being.

ENERGY FIELDS AND CHAKRAS: The metaphysical body is composed of subtle energy fields that extend beyond the physical body, including the aura and energy centres known as chakras. The aura is an electromagnetic field that surrounds and interpenetrates the physical body, reflecting one's emotional, mental, and spiritual state. Chakras are spinning vortices of energy located along the central axis of the body, regulating the flow of life force energy (Prana or Qi) and influencing physical, emotional, and spiritual health (Judith, 2004).

CONSCIOUSNESS AND MIND-BODY CONNECTION: The metaphysical body encompasses consciousness, the awareness of one's existence and experience. Consciousness is not limited to the brain but is considered a fundamental aspect of the universe, permeating all levels of reality. The mind-body connection illustrates how thoughts, emotions, and beliefs can influence physical health and well-being, highlighting the interconnectedness of mental, emotional, and physical states (Dossey, 2013).

SPIRITUAL DIMENSIONS AND TRANSPERSONAL EXPERIENCES: The metaphysical body encompasses spiritual dimensions beyond ordinary perception, including experiences of transcendence, unity, and expanded consciousness. Transpersonal experiences, such as mystical states, near-death experiences, and spiritual awakening, provide glimpses into the interconnected nature of reality and the existence of a higher or universal consciousness (Grof, 2006).

HOLISTIC HEALING AND ENERGY MODALITIES: Holistic healing modalities acknowledge the existence of the metaphysical body and seek to restore balance and harmony on physical, emotional, and spiritual levels. Practices such as acupuncture, Reiki, yoga, meditation, and energy medicine work with the body's subtle energy fields to promote healing, relaxation, and spiritual growth. These modalities recognise the interconnectedness of mind, body, and spirit and aim to address imbalances at their root (Eden, 2008).

CULTIVATING AWARENESS AND INTEGRATION: Cultivating awareness of the metaphysical body involves developing mindfulness, intuition, and spiritual practices that deepen one's understanding of self and the interconnectedness of all beings. Through practices such as meditation, breath work, and self-inquiry, individuals can explore the depths of their consciousness and awaken to the inherent wholeness and divinity within themselves and the universe.

CONCLUSION

The metaphysical body encompasses dimensions of human existence beyond the physical realm, including energy fields, consciousness, and spiritual dimensions. Understanding and exploring the metaphysical body offer pathways to healing, transformation, and spiritual evolution, inviting individuals to embrace the interconnectedness of mind, body, and spirit in their journey of self-discovery and growth.

Cultural Philosophies of the Energy Body

Throughout history, diverse cultural philosophies have conceptualised the human energy body in unique and intricate ways, reflecting varied belief systems and traditions. From ancient Eastern philosophies to indigenous practices worldwide, the concept of the energy body has been central to understanding health, spirituality, and the interconnectedness of all beings.

IN TRADITIONAL CHINESE MEDICINE (TCM), the concept of Qi (pronounced "chee") forms the cornerstone of understanding the human energy body. Qi is believed to flow through meridians, channels that connect various organs and systems, maintaining balance and vitality within the body (Jahnke, 2002). Practices such as acupuncture and qigong aim to regulate Qi flow to restore health and harmony.

SIMILARLY, Ayurveda, the ancient healing system of India, recognises the vital force known as Prana. Prana is thought to permeate all levels of existence, including the physical, mental, and spiritual realms. In Ayurvedic philosophy, imbalances in Prana can lead to disease, and practices like yoga and pranayama are used to optimise Pranic flow and promote well-being (Lad, 1999).

INDIGENOUS CULTURES worldwide also hold unique perspectives on the human energy body. For example, among the Navajo people of North America, the concept of Hózhó encompasses beauty, harmony, and balance in both the physical and spiritual realms. According to Navajo beliefs, every living being possesses a unique life force or energy body, which interconnects with the natural world and the cosmos. This energy body is intricately linked to the individual's well-being, health, and spiritual vitality. Practices such as ceremony, prayer, and storytelling are employed to maintain Hózhó and ensure health and prosperity (Pinto, 2010).

MOREOVER, the Japanese tradition of Reiki offers insights into the human energy body as a system of subtle energy centres known as chakras. Reiki practitioners channel universal life force energy to balance and harmonise the chakras, facilitating healing and spiritual growth (Stein, 2003).

KUNDALINI PHILOSOPHY IS an ancient Indian tradition centred on awakening spiritual energy through practices like yoga and meditation. It involves the ascent of Kundalini energy through chakras along the spine, leading to heightened awareness and enlightenment.

IN CHRISTIANITY, the concept of the energy body is often approached through spiritual and theological perspectives rather than through explicit references to energy centre's or channels. The focus is primarily on the spiritual essence and the presence of the Holy Spirit within individuals. While Christianity may not directly use terminology like "chakras" or "energy body," the idea of spiritual energy and vitality is implicit in many Christian teachings.

CONCLUSION

Cultural philosophies of the human energy body provide rich insights into the interconnectedness of mind, body, and spirit. These diverse perspectives offer holistic approaches to health and well-being, emphasising the importance of balance, flow, and harmony within the energetic framework of the human experience.

Japanese Cultural Beliefs on Ki (Chi)

In Japanese culture, the concept of Ki, often synonymous with chi in Chinese culture, holds significant importance and deeply influences various aspects of life, health, and spirituality. Ki represents the fundamental life force energy that permeates the universe and animates all living beings. Understanding Japanese cultural beliefs surrounding Ki provides insights into traditional healing practices, martial arts, and spiritual disciplines.

KI IN TRADITIONAL JAPANESE PHILOSOPHY: Ki is regarded as the essential energy or life force that flows through all living things, including humans, animals, plants, and even inanimate objects. It is the underlying principle that sustains life and governs the dynamic balance of the universe (Ueshiba, 2019).

IN JAPANESE PHILOSOPHY, the concept of Ki is deeply rooted in Shintoism, Buddhism, and Taoism, influencing beliefs about health, nature, and the interconnectedness of all things.

KI IN TRADITIONAL HEALING ARTS: Traditional Japanese medicine, known as Kampo, emphasises the balance and harmonisation of Ki within the body to maintain health and prevent disease. Practices such as acupuncture, moxibustion, herbal medicine, and shiatsu massage are used to regulate the flow of Ki and restore balance to the body's energy system (Kuriyama, 1999).

REIKI, a Japanese healing technique developed in the early 20th century by Mikao Usui, harnesses the universal life force energy (Ki) to promote healing, relaxation, and spiritual growth. Reiki practitioners channel Ki through their hands to support the body's natural healing processes and restore energetic balance (Stein, 2003).

KI IN MARTIAL ARTS: In Japanese martial arts such as Aikido, Karate, and Kendo, the concept of Ki plays a central role in training and practice. Practitioners seek to cultivate and harness Ki to enhance their physical abilities, mental focus, and spiritual development (Stevens, 2010).

AIKIDO FOUNDER MORIHEI UESHIBA emphasised the importance of Ki in martial arts, teaching that true mastery comes from aligning one's Ki with the natural flow of energy and harmonising with the opponent's movements (Ueshiba, 2019).

KI IN SPIRITUAL PRACTICES: In Japanese spiritual traditions, such as Shinto and Zen Buddhism, Ki is revered as the vital essence that connects individuals to the divine and the natural world. Practices such as meditation, chanting, and mindfulness cultivate awareness of Ki and facilitate spiritual awakening (Suzuki, 2010).

ZEN MEDITATION (ZAZEN) emphasises the direct experience of Ki, encouraging practitioners to quiet the mind, transcend dualistic thinking, and perceive the interconnectedness of all phenomena (Suzuki, 2010).

CONCLUSION

Ki holds profound significance in Japanese culture, shaping beliefs about health, martial arts, and spirituality. By cultivating awareness of Ki and harmonising its flow within oneself and the environment, individuals can achieve greater health, vitality, and spiritual awakening.

Ancient Greek Cultural Beliefs about Pneuma

In ancient Greek culture, the concept of pneuma held profound significance, influencing beliefs about the nature of life, the cosmos, and the human soul. Pneuma, often translated as "breath" or "spirit," represented the vital force that permeated the universe and animated all living beings. Understanding ancient Greek cultural beliefs surrounding pneuma provides insights into philosophy, medicine, and spirituality during this period.

PHILOSOPHICAL PERSPECTIVES: In Greek philosophy, pneuma was central to the cosmological theories of pre-Socratic philosophers such as Anaximenes and Heraclitus. They proposed that pneuma was the primary substance from which all things emerged and to which they returned, emphasising its role as the underlying principle of existence (Frede, 1987).

STOIC PHILOSOPHERS, including Zeno of Citium and Chrysippus, further developed the concept of pneuma as the divine breath or animating force that permeated the cosmos. They believed that pneuma was responsible for the order and harmony of the universe, guiding the development of nature and the human soul (Inwood, 2007).

MEDICAL THEORY: In ancient Greek medicine, pneuma was associated with the breath, vitality, and life force within the body. Physicians such as Hippocrates and Galen described pneuma as a vital substance that circulated through the bloodstream, nourishing the organs and maintaining health (Rocca, 2004).

ACCORDING TO GALENIC MEDICINE, pneuma existed in three forms: natural pneuma, vital pneuma, and animal pneuma. Natural pneuma corresponded to the air breathed in from the environment, vital pneuma represented the breath of life, and animal pneuma was the subtle energy that circulated within the body (Hankinson, 1998).

SPIRITUAL AND RELIGIOUS SIGNIFICANCE: Pneuma also held religious and spiritual significance in ancient Greek religion and mythology. It was associated with divine breath and the animating force of the gods, symbolising their power and authority over the natural world (Dodds, 1951).

. . .

THE ORACLE OF DELPHI, one of the most revered religious sites in ancient Greece, was believed to be inspired by the pneuma of Apollo, the god of prophecy and wisdom. The priestess, known as the Pythia, inhaled vapours rising from a chasm in the earth, which were thought to convey Apollo's divine inspiration (Fontenrose, 1978).

CULTURAL EXPRESSIONS: Ancient Greek literature and art often depicted pneuma as a symbol of life, creativity, and divine inspiration. Poets such as Homer and Hesiod invoked pneuma in their epic poems to convey the breath of life and the animating force of the gods (Nagy, 1990).

GREEK ARTISTS REPRESENTED pneuma in sculptures and pottery, depicting divine beings and mythical figures imbued with vitality and vigour, symbolising the eternal cycle of life and death (Boardman, 2000).

CONCLUSION

Pneuma was a central concept in ancient Greek culture, encompassing philosophical, medical, spiritual, and artistic dimensions. Its multifaceted nature reflected the Greeks' profound understanding of the interconnectedness of the cosmos and the human experience, shaping their worldview and cultural expressions.

Meridians in Traditional Chinese Medicine

Traditional Chinese Medicine (TCM), originating from ancient Chinese philosophy and cultural beliefs, is a comprehensive system of healing that views the human body as a dynamic network of interconnected channels known as meridians. These meridians serve as pathways through which vital energy, known as Qi, flows to nourish and harmonise the body, mind, and spirit. Understanding the concept of meridians is essential for diagnosing and treating imbalances within the body and restoring health and well-being.

OVERVIEW OF MERIDIANS: Meridians are invisible channels that form a network throughout the body, connecting various organs, tissues, and systems. There are twelve primary meridians, each associated with a specific organ system, as well as numerous secondary meridians and collaterals (Maciocia, 2015).

QI, the life force energy, flows continuously through the meridians, maintaining balance and vitality within the body. When Qi becomes blocked or disrupted, disharmony and disease can arise.

TYPES OF MERIDIANS:

- **Yin Meridians:** Yin meridians are associated with the internal organs and are characterised by their nourishing, cooling, and inward-moving qualities. The Yin meridians include the Heart, Lung, Spleen, Kidney, Pericardium, and Liver meridians.

- **Yang Meridians:** Yang meridians are associated with the external structures of the body and exhibit warming, activating, and outward-moving qualities. The Yang meridians include the Small Intestine, Large Intestine, Stomach, Bladder, Triple Burner, and Gallbladder meridians (Maciocia, 2015).

FUNCTIONS OF MERIDIANS:

Regulating Qi and Blood: Meridians govern the flow of Qi and blood throughout the body, ensuring proper circulation and nourishment of tissues and organs.

CONNECTING INTERNAL AND EXTERNAL: Meridians serve as bridges between the internal organs and external body structures, integrating physiological functions with sensory perception and movement.

INFLUENCING HEALTH AND DISEASE: Imbalances or blockages in the meridians can lead to various health issues, including pain, inflammation, digestive disorders, and emotional disturbances.

PROVIDING DIAGNOSTIC AND TREATMENT FRAMEWORK: TCM practitioners diagnose imbalances by assessing the flow of Qi and blood within the meridians and use acupuncture, herbal medicine, massage, and qigong to restore balance and promote healing (Kaptchuk, 2002).

. . .

ACUPUNCTURE AND MERIDIAN THERAPY: Acupuncture is a key therapeutic modality in TCM that involves the insertion of fine needles into specific points along the meridians to stimulate Qi flow, alleviate pain, and restore health. Acupuncture points are carefully selected based on the patient's symptoms, constitution, and meridian imbalances.

MERIDIAN THERAPY also includes techniques such as moxibustion, cupping, gua sha, and acupressure, which work to balance the flow of Qi and blood within the meridians and promote healing (Nielsen et al., 2005).

CONCLUSION

Meridians form the foundation of Traditional Chinese Medicine, providing a framework for understanding the body's energetic anatomy and promoting health and well-being. By harmonising the flow of Qi within the meridians, individuals can cultivate balance, vitality, and resilience in body, mind, and spirit.

Understanding the Ayurvedic Energetic Body

Ayurveda, the ancient system of holistic medicine originating from the Indian subcontinent, offers profound insights into the energetic body, known as "prana" or "life force energy." Central to Ayurvedic philosophy is the concept that all living beings possess a unique combination of the five elements: earth, water, fire, air, and space. These elements manifest in the physical body and also in subtle energetic forms.

· · ·

THE THREE DOSHAS: Vata, Pitta, and Kapha

Ayurveda categorises the human body and mind into three primary constitutions or doshas: Vata, Pitta, and Kapha. Each dosha represents a combination of the elements and governs specific physiological and psychological functions. Vata is associated with air and space, responsible for movement and communication within the body. Pitta, governed by fire and water, controls metabolism, digestion, and transformation. Kapha, influenced by earth and water, governs structure, stability, and nourishment.

PRANA: The Vital Life Force

In Ayurveda, prana is the vital life force that animates all living beings. It is the subtle energy that permeates the entire universe and sustains life. Prana flows through the body via channels known as nadis, similar to the concept of meridians in traditional Chinese medicine. When prana is balanced and freely flowing, it promotes health, vitality, and well-being. However, imbalances or blockages in prana can lead to disease and disharmony.

BALANCING the Energetic Body

Ayurveda offers various practices to balance and harmonise the energetic body. These include:

- **Pranayama:** Breathing techniques and exercises designed to regulate and enhance the flow of prana in the body.

- **Yoga:** Asanas (postures) and movements that promote physical strength, flexibility, and energetic alignment.
- **Meditation:** Practices to quiet the mind, cultivate awareness, and connect with the subtle realms of consciousness.
- **Ayurvedic Diet and Lifestyle:** Emphasising the importance of wholesome nutrition, proper digestion, adequate rest, and regular daily routines to support optimal energy flow and balance.

Conclusion

The Ayurvedic understanding of the energetic body provides a holistic framework for promoting health, vitality, and spiritual growth. By cultivating awareness of prana and working to balance the doshas, individuals can enhance their overall well-being and harmonise with the natural rhythms of existence.

Kundalini Energy and Dimensions of Consciousness

Kundalini, is a potent and transformative energy believed to reside at the base of the spine, central to various spiritual traditions, a concept deeply rooted in ancient Indian spiritual traditions, particularly Hinduism and Tantra.

THE PATH TO ENLIGHTENMENT: In Kundalini belief, individuals are conditioned to exist within a negative plane, characterised by limited consciousness and attachment to ego-driven patterns. Awakening the dormant Kundalini energy at the base of the spine is considered the path to enlightenment.

· · ·

PRACTICES FOR KUNDALINI AWAKENING: Through yoga, meditation, and mindful living, individuals raise Kundalini energy through the chakras, unlocking higher states of consciousness and transcending ego limitations. Kundalini teachings emphasise the importance of self-awareness, inner transformation, and the cultivation of spiritual wisdom to navigate the journey towards enlightenment (Sharma, 2019).

UTILISING SACRED TOOL: Songs, sacred chants and mantras (Kirtans) in Kundalini practices shift energy, elevate consciousness, and cultivate connection to the divine, facilitating inner liberation and enlightenment. These sacred chants and mantras used in Kundalini yoga practice often invoke themes of love, light, and spiritual transformation, serving as powerful tools for inner liberation and enlightenment.

TRANSCENDING **Negativity - Embodying Love and Light:** These transformative practices enable individuals to transcend negativity, expand awareness, and embody love and light, fostering spiritual growth and well-being.

EXPLORING **Kundalini Dimensions - Insights into Consciousness:** Kundalini awakening initiates a profound shift in consciousness, expanding awareness beyond ego limitations and facilitating spiritual evolution. As Kundalini ascends through the chakras, individuals may experience various dimensions of consciousness.

. . .

THE NATURE of Kundalini Energy and Consciousness:
Kundalini is depicted as a coiled serpent symbolising latent spiritual potential. When awakened, it ascends through subtle
energy channels, activating chakras and purifying mind, body,
and spirit (Satyananda Saraswati, 1984). The chakras correspond
to different dimensions of consciousness, serving as gateways to
higher awareness and self-realisation (Judith, 2004). Kundalini
awakening leads to heightened awareness, transcendent experiences, and spiritual evolution, guiding individuals on the path to
self-realisation (White, 2000).

INTEGRATION AND TRANSFORMATION: Kundalini awakening and
integration require patience, dedication, and surrender.
Through self-awareness and mindfulness practices, individuals
align with their true nature and realise their highest potential
(Krishna, 1993).

CONCLUSION

In conclusion, Kundalini energy serves as a transformative
force deeply embedded in ancient Indian spiritual traditions,
offering a pathway to enlightenment and heightened consciousness. Through practices like yoga, meditation, and sacred
chants, individuals awaken Kundalini energy, transcending ego
limitations and embodying love and light. This journey of spiritual evolution unlocks profound insights into consciousness and
leads to integration and transformation, fostering alignment
with one's true nature and highest potential.

Christian Cultural Philosophies of the Energy Body

While Christianity does not have a singular cultural philosophy in the same way that systems like Traditional Chinese Medicine or Ayurveda do, its principles and practices are deeply ingrained in cultural contexts where it is practiced.

IN CHRISTIANITY, the concept of the energy body is often approached through spiritual and theological perspectives rather than through explicit references to energy centres or channels. The focus is primarily on the spiritual essence and the presence of the Holy Spirit within individuals. While Christianity may not directly use terminology like "chakras" or "energy body," the idea of spiritual energy and vitality is implicit in many Christian teachings.

THE HOLY SPIRIT and Spiritual Vitality: Central to Christian beliefs is the concept of the Holy Spirit, often described as the divine presence of God within believers. In Christian theology, the Holy Spirit is considered the source of spiritual vitality and empowerment. It is believed to dwell within individuals who have accepted Jesus Christ as their saviour, guiding them in their spiritual journey and empowering them to live according to God's will (John 14:16-17).

PRAYER, Healing, and Spiritual Renewal: Christian practices such as prayer, laying on of hands, and anointing with oil are seen as channels through which spiritual energy and healing power flow. In Christian traditions, prayer is not only a means of communication with God but also a conduit for receiving divine grace and spiritual renewal. Through prayer, Christians seek spiritual strength, healing, and restoration of the body, mind, and spirit (James 5:14-15).

SACRAMENTS AND SPIRITUAL TRANSFORMATION: Sacraments such as baptism and communion are believed to be sacred rituals through which individuals experience spiritual transformation and renewal. Baptism is viewed as a symbol of spiritual rebirth and initiation into the Christian community, while communion represents the spiritual nourishment and communion with Christ's body and blood (1 Corinthians 11:23-26).

CONCLUSION

Christian cultural perspectives illuminate the energy body, focusing on spiritual vitality and transformation. While not explicitly addressing energy centres, Christianity emphasises the Holy Spirit's presence and guidance, prayer, and sacraments for spiritual renewal. Believers view the Holy Spirit as the source of empowerment, guiding them in their faith journey. Through prayer and sacraments like baptism and communion, individuals experience spiritual rebirth, nourishment, and communion with the divine, fostering spiritual growth within Christian traditions.

4

THE ENERGETIC BODY, FIELDS AND DIMENSIONS

The Energy Body

Within the human body lies not only its physical form but also its energetic counterpart, representing the subtle or metaphysical dimension. In preceding sections, we briefly discussed various cultural beliefs regarding the flow of energy within the body. In this section, our exploration will turn to the concept of energy centres, known as chakras, which are akin to the organs within the physical body. Our aim is to delve deeper into the realm of chakra energy centres.

An Overview of Energy Centres (Chakras)

Chakras are vital energy centres within the human body that play a crucial role in regulating physical, emotional, and spiritual well-being. Originating from ancient Indian spiritual traditions, the concept of chakras has gained popularity in various holistic healing practices worldwide. Understanding the nature and function of chakras can provide profound insights into the holistic nature of human existence.

OVERVIEW OF CHAKRAS: In Sanskrit, the word "chakra" translates to "wheel" or "disk," symbolising the spinning vortex of energy at each chakra point. Traditionally, there are seven main chakras aligned along the spine, from the base to the crown of the head. Each chakra is associated with specific physical, emotional, and spiritual attributes, representing different aspects of human experience (Judith, 2004).

CHAKRA SYSTEM AND ENERGY FLOW: The chakra system serves as a network through which life force energy, known as Prana in Hinduism, flows throughout the body. When the chakras are open, balanced, and aligned, energy flows freely, promoting health, vitality, and spiritual growth. However, blockages or imbalances in the chakras can lead to physical ailments, emotional disturbances, and spiritual stagnation (Dale, 2001).

SEVEN MAIN CHAKRAS:

- **Root Chakra (Muladhara):** Located at the base of the spine, the root chakra governs feelings of safety, security, and survival instincts.
- **Sacral Chakra (Svadhisthana):** Positioned in the lower abdomen, the sacral chakra is associated with creativity, pleasure, and emotional well-being.
- **Solar Plexus Chakra (Manipura):** Situated in the upper abdomen, the solar plexus chakra governs personal power, self-esteem, and confidence.

- **Heart Chakra (Anahata):** Located in the centre of the chest, the heart chakra is associated with love, compassion, and emotional balance.
- **Throat Chakra (Vishuddha):** Positioned in the throat area, the throat chakra governs communication, self-expression, and authenticity.
- **Third Eye Chakra (Ajna):** Located between the eyebrows, the third eye chakra is associated with intuition, insight, and spiritual awareness.
- **Crown Chakra (Sahasrara):** Situated at the top of the head, the crown chakra represents higher consciousness, divine connection, and enlightenment.

Balancing and Healing Chakras: Various practices are used to balance and heal the chakras, including meditation, visualisation, yoga, breath work, sound therapy, and energy healing techniques like Reiki. These practices aim to remove blockages, restore energy flow, and promote harmony within the chakra system (Eden, 2008).

Integration into Holistic Healing: Understanding chakras provides a holistic framework for addressing physical, emotional, and spiritual imbalances. By working with the chakras, individuals can cultivate greater self-awareness, emotional resilience, and spiritual growth, leading to a more balanced and fulfilling life.

Conclusion

Understanding chakras offers profound insights into the interconnectedness of mind, body, and spirit. By harmonising and balancing the chakra system, individuals can cultivate vibrant health, emotional well-being, and spiritual awakening.

Harmonising and Balancing the Energy Body

Achieving harmony and balance within the energy body is a fundamental aspect of many holistic health practices. From ancient traditions to modern techniques, various methods are employed to align and optimise the flow of energy, promoting overall well-being and vitality.

MEDITATION AND MINDFULNESS: Meditation practices, such as mindfulness meditation and loving-kindness meditation, are effective tools for harmonising the energy body. By cultivating present-moment awareness and inner peace, meditation helps to release blockages and restore balance within the energetic system (Chiesa & Malinowski, 2011).

YOGA AND TAI CHI: Yoga and Tai Chi are ancient movement-based practices that integrate breath, movement, and meditation to promote balance and harmony within the body and mind. These practices help to open energy channels, release tension, and cultivate a sense of flow and vitality (Wang et al., 2016).

ACUPUNCTURE AND ACUPRESSURE: Derived from traditional Chinese medicine, acupuncture and acupressure aim to balance the flow of Qi (life force energy) through the body's meridian system. By stimulating specific acupoints, these therapies regulate energy flow, alleviate symptoms, and promote overall health and well-being (Vickers et al., 2012).

. . .

SOUND HEALING: Sound healing utilises the vibrational qualities of sound to harmonise and balance the energy body. Techniques such as chanting, singing bowls, and tuning forks resonate with the body's energy centres, promoting relaxation, stress reduction, and energetic alignment (Wang & van Oudenhove, 2020).

ENERGY WORK AND REIKI: Energy healing modalities like Reiki, Healing Touch, and Pranic Healing work with the body's subtle energy fields to restore balance and vitality. Practitioners channel universal life force energy to clear blockages, remove stagnant energy, and support the body's natural healing processes (Baldwin et al., 2013).

NATURE CONNECTION: Spending time in nature and connecting with the natural world is essential for harmonising the energy body. Nature provides a source of grounding, rejuvenation, and energetic nourishment, helping to restore balance and vitality on physical, emotional, and spiritual levels (Mayer et al., 2009).

CONCLUSION: Harmonising and balancing the energy body is a multifaceted process that encompasses various practices and techniques. By integrating mindfulness, movement, energy work, and connection with nature, individuals can cultivate vibrant health, inner peace, and spiritual well-being.

Blocked Chakras and Their Effects

Blocked chakras can significantly impact both the mind and body, leading to a range of physical, emotional, and spiritual imbalances. The chakra system serves as a vital energy network within the human body, and when blockages occur, the flow of energy becomes restricted, affecting overall well-being. Recognising the signs of blocked chakras and implementing effective techniques to unblock them are essential steps toward restoring harmony and vitality.

EFFECTS OF BLOCKED CHAKRAS:

Physical Effects: Blocked chakras can manifest as various physical symptoms, including chronic pain, fatigue, digestive issues, and compromised immune function. Each chakra is associated with specific organs and bodily systems, and blockages in these energy centres can disrupt their functioning (Dale, 2001).

Emotional Effects: Blocked chakras can also give rise to emotional disturbances such as anxiety, depression, irritability, and emotional numbness. Emotional energy becomes stagnant when chakras are blocked, leading to an imbalance in mood, behaviour, and interpersonal relationships.

Spiritual Effects: On a spiritual level, blocked chakras can hinder personal growth, intuition, and spiritual connection. Individuals may feel disconnected from their higher purpose, lacking a sense of meaning, fulfilment, and inner peace.

IDENTIFYING BLOCKED CHAKRAS: Understanding the signs and symptoms associated with each chakra can help identify areas of imbalance within the energy system. For example, a blocked root chakra may manifest as feelings of insecurity, financial instability, or a lack of grounding, while a blocked throat chakra could result in difficulty expressing oneself or communicating effectively (Judith, 2004).

Techniques to Unblock Chakras:

- **Meditation:** Mindfulness meditation and chakra meditation techniques can help to release energetic blockages and restore balance within the chakra system. Focusing on each chakra individually, practitioners visualise healing energy flowing freely through the energy centres, clearing away obstacles and promoting vitality (Eden, 2008).

- **Energy Healing:** Modalities like Reiki, Healing Touch, and Pranic Healing involve the channeling of universal life force energy to remove blockages and restore harmony within the chakras. Energy healers use hands-on or hands-off techniques to balance the energy field, facilitating healing on physical, emotional, and spiritual levels (Baldwin et al., 2013).

- **Yoga and Movement:** Practicing yoga asanas specifically designed to stimulate and balance the chakras can help release tension and stagnant energy from the body. Poses like forward bends, twists, and heart-opening postures target specific chakra points, promoting energy flow and alignment (Frawley & Summerfield Kozak, 2002).

- **Sound Therapy:** Sound healing techniques, including chanting, singing bowls, and tuning forks, utilise vibrational frequencies to harmonise the chakras and promote energetic balance. Sound vibrations resonate with the body's energy centres, helping to release blockages and restore vitality (Wang & van Oudenhove, 2020).

CONCLUSION

Understanding and addressing blocked chakras are essential for achieving holistic well-being and vitality. By identifying signs of imbalance, practicing mindfulness, and utilising various healing modalities, individuals can release energetic blockages, restore harmony within the chakra system, and cultivate a greater sense of health, balance, and inner peace.

Yoga Poses for Chakra Alignment

Yoga offers a holistic approach to balancing and aligning the chakras, integrating physical postures, breath work, and meditation to promote energetic harmony and vitality. By practicing specific yoga poses that target each chakra, individuals can release energetic blockages, stimulate energy flow, and cultivate a greater sense of well-being. Drawing from ancient yogic traditions and modern insights, these poses facilitate chakra alignment and support overall health and balance.

IT IS important to work within your abilities and avoid striving for what may be perceived as the 'perfect' posture. The journey of yoga is about gently opening up the body and honouring its current capabilities. By listening to your body and practicing with mindfulness, you can cultivate a deeper awareness of your physical and mental states, allowing for gradual progress and transformation.

GIVEN the multitude of yoga practices available, each tailored to address different needs and preferences, selecting the right one to enhance flexibility and strength becomes a personal journey. Below, we explore traditional poses utilised to release blockages in energy centres.

ROOT CHAKRA (MULADHARA)

- **Mountain Pose (Tadasana):** Grounding and stabilising, Mountain Pose connects practitioners with the earth, fostering a sense of rootedness and security.
- **Tree Pose (Vrksasana):** By balancing on one leg, Tree Pose helps to strengthen the legs and activate the root chakra, enhancing feelings of stability and connection to the earth (Iyengar, 2001).

Sacral Chakra (Svadhisthana)

- **Bound Angle Pose (Baddha Konasana):** Opening the hips and pelvis, Bound Angle Pose stimulates the sacral chakra, encouraging creativity, emotional expression, and sensuality.
- **Cobra Pose (Bhujangasana):** Backbends like Cobra Pose help to awaken the energy of the sacral chakra, promoting flexibility, flow, and vitality in the lower abdomen (Stephens, 2010).

Solar Plexus Chakra (Manipura)

- **Boat Pose (Navasana):** Strengthening the core and abdominal muscles, Boat Pose activates the solar plexus chakra, fostering a sense of personal power, confidence, and self-esteem.
- **Warrior III (Virabhadrasana III):** Balancing on one leg, Warrior III cultivates strength and stability, empowering practitioners to access their inner strength and assertiveness (Iyengar, 2001).

Heart Chakra (Anahata)

- **Bridge Pose (Setu Bandhasana):** Opening the chest and heart centre, Bridge Pose expands the heart chakra, promoting love, compassion, and emotional balance.
- **Camel Pose (Ustrasana):** Backbends like Camel Pose stretch the front body and open the heart, encouraging vulnerability, forgiveness, and connection (Stephens, 2010).

Throat Chakra (Vishuddha)

- **Fish Pose (Matsyasana):** Opening the throat and chest, Fish Pose stimulates the throat chakra, enhancing communication, self-expression, and authenticity.
- **Plow Pose (Halasana):** Inversion poses like Plow Pose activate the throat chakra, encouraging introspection, clarity, and truthful expression (Iyengar, 2001).

Third Eye Chakra (Ajna)

- **Child's Pose (Balasana):** Resting the forehead on the mat, Child's Pose invites introspection and inner focus, stimulating the third eye chakra and enhancing intuition and insight.

- **Downward-Facing Dog (Adho Mukha Svanasana):** Inverted and grounding, Downward-Facing Dog calms the mind, relieves tension, and activates the third eye chakra, fostering clarity and concentration (Stephens, 2010).

Crown Chakra (Sahasrara)

- **Headstand (Sirsasana):** Known as the king of yoga poses, Headstand activates the crown chakra, promoting spiritual connection, higher consciousness, and enlightenment.

- **Lotus Pose (Padmasana):** Sitting in Lotus Pose, practitioners cultivate a sense of inner peace, tranquility, and divine connection, aligning with the energy of the crown chakra (Iyengar, 2001).

Conclusion

INCORPORATING yoga can support chakra alignment and promote holistic well-being, fostering balance, vitality, and spiritual growth. It is essential to remember that the journey of yoga extends beyond physical postures; it encompasses a deep connection with oneself and the subtle energies within. By practicing with mindfulness and self-awareness, individuals can cultivate a deeper understanding of their bodies, minds, and spirits, facilitating profound transformation and inner harmony. As you explore the diverse landscape of yoga, remember to honour your body's unique capabilities and embrace the journey of self-discovery with compassion and patience.

MAY your practice be a source of inspiration, healing, and empowerment as you continue to evolve on your path towards wholeness and well-being.

Understanding the Energetic Field

The concept of the energetic field surrounding the human body, often referred to as the biofield or the body's electromagnetic field, has been the subject of scientific research in various disciplines, including bioelectromagnetics, biophysics, and alternative medicine. While there is ongoing research in this area, it is important to note that the scientific understanding of the human energy field is still evolving, and there is debate within the scientific community regarding its nature and properties.

THE ENERGETIC FIELD, also known as the biofield or aura, is an invisible, electromagnetic field that surrounds and interpenetrates the human body. It is composed of subtle energies, vibrations, and information that emanate from the body's cells, organs, and energy centres (Popp et al., 1988).

THE ENERGETIC FIELD extends beyond the physical body, forming a dynamic interface between the individual and the external environment. It acts as a bridge between the material and spiritual realms, reflecting the interconnectedness of all living beings (Oschman, 2000).

CHARACTERISTICS OF THE ENERGETIC FIELD: The energetic field is characterised by its multidimensional nature, encompassing physical, emotional, mental, and spiritual aspects of being. It is comprised of various layers, each corresponding to different levels of consciousness and subtle energy dynamics (Brennan, 1988).

. . .

THE COLOURS, patterns, and densities of the energetic field reflect the individual's state of health, emotions, thoughts, and spiritual evolution. Imbalances, blockages, or disturbances in the energetic field can manifest as physical illness, emotional distress, or spiritual disconnection (Gerber, 2001).

ENERGETIC FIELD AND HEALTH: In holistic healing traditions, the energetic field is regarded as the primary matrix of health and vitality. It serves as a blueprint for physical well-being, influencing cellular function, organ integrity, and systemic balance (Mills et al., 2005).

PRACTICES SUCH AS ENERGY MEDICINE, acupuncture, Reiki, and qigong work with the energetic field to restore harmony, clear blockages, and promote self-healing. By rebalancing the flow of energy, these modalities support holistic health and well-being (Eden, 2008).

ENERGETIC FIELD AND CONSCIOUSNESS: The energetic field is intimately linked to consciousness, serving as a vehicle for self-awareness, intuition, and spiritual growth. It reflects the individual's level of consciousness, awareness, and alignment with higher states of being (Talbot, 1991).

SPIRITUAL PRACTICES SUCH AS MEDITATION, mindfulness, and energy work cultivate greater sensitivity to the energetic field, expanding perception, intuition, and connection to the divine. Through inner exploration, individuals can deepen their understanding of the energetic nature of reality (Wilber, 2000).

. . .

Implications for Interconnectedness: The energetic field transcends individual boundaries, encompassing the collective consciousness of humanity and the interconnected web of life. It reflects the interdependence and interrelationship of all beings, fostering compassion, empathy, and unity (Dossey, 1999).

By recognising the interconnected nature of the energetic field, individuals can cultivate a sense of shared responsibility and stewardship for the well-being of the planet and all its inhabitants. Collective healing and transformation become possible through conscious co-creation and harmonious collaboration (Sheldrake, 1981).

Conclusion

The energetic field offers a profound lens through which to explore the mysteries of existence and the interconnectedness of all things. By deepening our understanding of the energetic field, we can awaken to the inherent unity of life and embrace the transformative power of conscious evolution.

Exploring Energetic Dimensions

Energetic dimensions represent the subtle layers of reality beyond the physical realm, where vibrations, frequencies, and consciousness interplay to shape the universe. Understanding energetic dimensions offers insights into the interconnectedness of all existence and the expansive nature of reality.

SUBTLE ENERGY FIELDS: Energetic dimensions encompass subtle energy fields that permeate the universe, including the electro-magnetic spectrum, quantum fields, and bioenergetic fields. These energy fields interact with each other and with conscious-ness, influencing the dynamics of the physical and non-physical realms.

VIBRATIONAL FREQUENCIES: Vibrational frequencies are fundamental to energetic dimensions, determining the qualities and characteristics of different states of consciousness and real-ity. Everything in the universe vibrates at a specific frequency, from subatomic particles to galaxies, and these vibrations give rise to diverse forms and expressions of energy and matter.

HIGHER STATES OF CONSCIOUSNESS: Energetic dimensions encompass higher states of consciousness beyond ordinary waking awareness, including expanded states of awareness, altered states of consciousness, and mystical experiences. These states of consciousness offer glimpses into the interconnected-ness of all things and the underlying unity of existence.

.   .   .

INTERCONNECTION OF MIND, **Body, and Spirit:** Energetic dimensions highlight the interconnection of mind, body, and spirit, illustrating how thoughts, emotions, and beliefs influence energetic patterns and physical manifestations. Practices such as meditation, yoga, and energy healing work with these energetic dimensions to promote health, balance, and spiritual growth.

SPIRITUAL REALMS AND ENTITIES: Energetic dimensions encompass spiritual realms and entities that exist beyond the physical plane, including angels, spirit guides, and higher-dimensional beings. These entities may serve as guides, teachers, and sources of wisdom and inspiration on the spiritual path.

QUANTUM CONSCIOUSNESS: Energetic dimensions intersect with the principles of quantum physics, revealing the interconnected nature of reality and the role of consciousness in shaping the universe. Quantum consciousness suggests that consciousness is fundamental to the fabric of reality, influencing the observation, measurement, and manifestation of physical phenomena.

TRANSPERSONAL EXPERIENCES: Energetic dimensions encompass transpersonal experiences that transcend individual identity and ego boundaries, such as mystical states, near-death experiences, and spiritual awakening. These experiences provide direct insights into the nature of reality and the existence of higher or expanded dimensions of consciousness.

CONCLUSION

Exploring energetic dimensions offers a deeper understanding of the nature of reality and the interconnectedness of
all existence. By embracing the expansive nature of energetic
dimensions, individuals can awaken to the inherent unity and
divinity within themselves and the universe.

Metaphysical Dimensions

Metaphysical dimensions refer to realms of existence beyond
the physical universe, where consciousness, energy, and spiritual
forces shape reality in ways that transcend ordinary perception.
Understanding metaphysical dimensions invites us to explore
the deeper layers of existence and the interconnectedness of all
things.

CONSCIOUSNESS AS FOUNDATION: At the core of metaphysical
dimensions lies consciousness, the fundamental aspect of existence that underlies all phenomena. Consciousness transcends
individual identity and ego, representing the universal awareness that permeates the cosmos and gives rise to the fabric of
reality.

NON-PHYSICAL REALMS: Metaphysical dimensions encompass
non-physical realms that exist beyond the limitations of space
and time. These realms include spiritual planes, higher dimensions, and alternate realities where subtle energies and spiritual
beings interact and manifest.

.   .   .

SUBTLE ENERGIES AND VIBRATIONAL FREQUENCIES: Subtle energies and vibrational frequencies are integral to metaphysical dimensions, shaping the qualities and characteristics of different states of reality. Everything in the universe vibrates at a specific frequency, and these vibrations interact with consciousness to create diverse forms and expressions of energy and matter.

INTERCONNECTEDNESS OF ALL EXISTENCE: Metaphysical dimensions reveal the interconnectedness of all existence, illustrating how every aspect of the universe is intricately linked and influenced by the underlying fabric of consciousness. This interconnectedness highlights the holistic nature of reality and the inherent unity of all creation.

EXPLORATION AND SPIRITUAL GROWTH: Exploring metaphysical dimensions offers pathways to spiritual growth, self-discovery, and transformation. Practices such as meditation, visualisation, and energy work enable individuals to access higher states of consciousness and connect with the deeper aspects of their being.

TRANSCENDENCE OF DUALISTIC THINKING: Metaphysical dimensions challenge dualistic thinking and linear concepts of time and space, inviting us to transcend limited perspectives and embrace the wholeness of existence. In these dimensions, concepts of past, present, and future merge into a timeless continuum, and boundaries between self and other dissolve.

. . .

INTEGRATION OF MULTIDIMENSIONAL AWARENESS: Embracing metaphysical dimensions involves integrating multidimensional awareness into everyday life, recognising the interconnectedness of physical, emotional, mental, and spiritual aspects of existence. This integration fosters a deeper sense of harmony, balance, and alignment with the higher purpose of existence.

CONCLUSION

Exploring metaphysical dimensions expands our understanding of reality and opens doors to profound experiences of interconnectedness, unity, and spiritual awakening. By delving into these dimensions, individuals can embark on a journey of self-discovery, transformation, and conscious evolution.

Dimensions of Consciousness

Consciousness, the essence of our being and experience, is a multifaceted phenomenon that transcends conventional understanding. In exploring the dimensions of consciousness, we delve into the various levels, states, and aspects of awareness that shape our perception of reality and our relationship with the universe.

LEVELS OF CONSCIOUSNESS: Consciousness exists on multiple levels, ranging from the subconscious and unconscious to the conscious and superconscious. Freudian psychology introduced the idea of the subconscious mind, which harbours repressed memories, desires, and instincts. Carl Jung expanded this concept to include the collective unconscious, a reservoir of archetypal symbols and patterns shared by humanity (Freud, 1915; Jung, 1959).

. . .

THE CONSCIOUS MIND represents our waking awareness and ability to perceive, think, and act in the present moment. The superconscious, or higher self, transcends individual identity and ego, connecting us to universal wisdom, intuition, and spiritual guidance (Assagioli, 1973).

STATES OF CONSCIOUSNESS: Consciousness fluctuates between different states, ranging from ordinary waking consciousness to altered states induced by meditation, dreams, psychedelics, and mystical experiences. William James categorised these states as normal waking consciousness (NWC), the stream of ordinary waking awareness, and altered states of consciousness (ASC), which involve shifts in perception, attention, and self-awareness (James, 1902).

ALTERED STATES of consciousness encompass a spectrum of experiences, including trance states, lucid dreaming, out-of-body experiences (OBEs), near-death experiences (NDEs), and mystical states of unity and transcendence (Tart, 1975).

DIMENSIONS OF CONSCIOUSNESS: The dimensions of consciousness extend beyond the physical realm, encompassing subtle planes, higher dimensions, and spiritual realms of existence. Theosophical teachings describe seven planes of consciousness, ranging from the physical plane to the divine or spiritual plane (Leadbeater & Besant, 1895).

. . .

QUANTUM PHYSICS SUGGESTS the existence of multiple dimensions beyond the three-dimensional space-time continuum, including higher-dimensional spaces and parallel universes that defy conventional notions of reality (Greene, 1999).

TRANSCENDENCE AND UNITY CONSCIOUSNESS: Transcendent experiences involve a shift in consciousness beyond ordinary perception and egoic identity, leading to profound states of unity, interconnectedness, and oneness with the cosmos. Unity consciousness represents the realisation that all beings are interconnected and inseparable manifestations of the same divine source (Wilber, 2000).

TRANSPERSONAL PSYCHOLOGY EXPLORES the transformative potential of transcendence, recognising it as a catalyst for personal growth, healing, and spiritual awakening (Walsh & Vaughan, 1993).

CONCLUSION

Exploring the dimensions of consciousness reveals the vast and intricate tapestry of human experience and existence. By embracing the myriad levels, states, and aspects of consciousness, we embark on a journey of self-discovery, growth, and transformation that transcends the boundaries of the known and expands our understanding of reality.

Exploring Spiritual Dimensions Across Cultures

Spiritual dimensions represent realms of existence beyond the physical, where individuals connect with higher consciousness, divine beings, and the cosmic order. Across diverse cultures and traditions, the concept of spiritual dimensions manifests in various forms, each offering unique insights into the nature of reality and the human experience.

EASTERN TRADITIONS: In Eastern traditions such as Hinduism, Buddhism, and Taoism, the concept of spiritual dimensions is central to understanding the nature of existence. Hinduism emphasises the idea of Loka, or cosmic planes, which include realms inhabited by gods, demigods, ancestors, and celestial beings. These realms exist in parallel to the physical world and are accessible through spiritual practices such as meditation, devotion, and ritual (Flood, 1996).

BUDDHISM INTRODUCES the concept of multiple realms of existence, known as the Six Realms, which represent different states of consciousness and karma. These realms include the realms of gods, demigods, humans, animals, hungry ghosts, and hell beings, each characterised by specific mental and emotional qualities (Gyatso, 1992).

TAOISM, on the other hand, describes the Dao, or the Way, as the underlying principle of the universe. The Dao encompasses both the physical and spiritual dimensions, representing the source of all existence and the path to spiritual enlightenment (Laozi, 6th century BCE).

. . .

INDIGENOUS CULTURES: Indigenous cultures around the world recognise the existence of spiritual dimensions that interpenetrate the physical realm. In Native American traditions, for example, the concept of the Spirit World encompasses realms inhabited by spirit guides, ancestors, and nature spirits. Shamans and medicine people serve as intermediaries between the physical and spiritual dimensions, facilitating healing, guidance, and communion with the unseen realms (Harner, 1982).

SIMILARLY, Australian Aboriginal spirituality emphasises the interconnectedness of all living beings and the Dreamtime, a spiritual dimension where ancestral beings created the landscape, laws, and rituals of the world. Dreamtime stories and ceremonies serve to maintain harmony and balance between the physical and spiritual dimensions (Berndt & Berndt, 1977).

WESTERN MYSTICISM: In Western mysticism and esoteric traditions, spiritual dimensions are often described in terms of planes of existence, levels of consciousness, and states of awareness. The Kabbalistic tradition in Judaism, for example, describes the Tree of Life, a symbolic representation of the divine emanations and spiritual realms. Each sephirot, or sphere, represents a different aspect of divine consciousness and spiritual evolution (Scholem, 1949).

CHRISTIAN MYSTICISM EXPLORES the idea of the Kingdom of God as a spiritual dimension that transcends earthly reality. Mystics such as Meister Eckhart and Teresa of Ávila describe experiences of divine union and mystical ecstasy, where the soul merges with the divine and glimpses the eternal truths of God (McGinn, 2006).

MODERN SPIRITUALITY: In contemporary spirituality, the concept of spiritual dimensions is explored through various practices such as meditation, energy healing, and consciousness expansion. New Age teachings and metaphysical beliefs posit the existence of higher vibrational dimensions, parallel realities, and ascended masters who guide humanity's evolution (Woolger & Woolger, 1988).

THE CONCEPT of the multiverse in quantum physics suggests the possibility of parallel universes and alternate dimensions beyond the observable universe. While scientific exploration of these dimensions remains speculative, it offers intriguing possibilities for understanding the nature of reality and consciousness (Greene, 2011).

BEYOND PERCEPTION: **Exploring Spiritual Dimensions**

In exploring spiritual dimensions across cultures, it becomes evident that these realms extend beyond our ordinary waking awareness. Just as energy vibrates at different frequencies, spiritual dimensions exist at varying levels of consciousness and vibrational frequencies. While our physical senses may not always perceive these dimensions directly, spiritual practices such as meditation, prayer, and energy work offer pathways to access higher states of consciousness and connect with these subtle realms. The vibrational nature of spiritual dimensions resonates with the idea that energetic frequency determines the scope of our perception and awareness, transcending the boundaries of the physical realm (Wilber, 2000). Through the lens of quantum physics, the concept of vibrational frequency finds resonance in the exploration of parallel universes and alternate dimensions, suggesting that reality extends far beyond what our senses perceive (Kaku, 2005). As we delve deeper into the exploration of spiritual dimensions, we uncover the interconnectedness of all existence and the vastness of the cosmic order.

Conclusion

In our exploration of spiritual dimensions across cultures, we find that these realms surpass our ordinary waking awareness. Embracing diverse traditions deepens our appreciation for spiritual complexity, revealing the universal quest for transcendence and connection to the divine.

Nurturing Intuition and Inner Knowing

Intuition, often referred to as inner knowing or gut feeling, is a profound aspect of human consciousness that transcends rational thought and arises from a deeper level of awareness. Understanding the process of intuition and learning how to enhance it can enrich our lives and guide us towards greater clarity, insight, and alignment with our true selves.

UNDERSTANDING INTUITION: Intuition is a form of non-linear, non-verbal intelligence that arises spontaneously from the subconscious mind. It provides insights, guidance, and solutions that may not be immediately evident through logical analysis or reasoning. Intuitive knowing often manifests as a subtle feeling, hunch, or inner voice that communicates messages from our higher self or the collective unconscious (Braud & Anderson, 1998).

THE PROCESS OF INTUITION: Intuition operates through a process of receptivity, attunement, and interpretation. It begins with cultivating inner stillness and receptivity to the subtle cues and impressions that arise within our awareness. By quieting the mind and opening ourselves to the present moment, we create space for intuitive insights to emerge.

ATTUNEMENT INVOLVES TUNING into our inner guidance system and paying attention to the sensations, emotions, and impressions that accompany intuitive knowing. This may involve sensing subtle shifts in energy, noticing bodily sensations, or receiving symbolic messages through dreams or synchronicities.

INTERPRETATION REQUIRES discernment and trust in the wisdom of our intuitive faculties. It involves deciphering the meaning behind intuitive messages and discerning whether they resonate with our deepest truths and values. Cultivating self-trust and confidence in our intuition allows us to act with clarity and conviction, even in the face of uncertainty (Vaughan, 1979).

ENHANCING INTUITION: There are several practices that can help enhance intuition and foster a deeper connection to our inner guidance:

- **Meditation and mindfulness:** Regular meditation practice cultivates inner stillness, clarity, and presence, making it easier to access intuitive insights and inner wisdom.

- Journaling and reflection: Keeping a journal and reflecting on our experiences, dreams, and intuitive impressions can help clarify and deepen our understanding of intuitive guidance.

- Creative expression: Engaging in creative activities such as art, music, or writing can stimulate intuitive insights and tap into the deeper currents of our subconscious mind.

- Nature connection: Spending time in nature and attuning to the rhythms and cycles of the natural world can heighten our intuitive sensitivity and deepen our connection to the web of life.

TRUSTING THE PROCESS: Trusting intuition is essential for harnessing its power and wisdom. This involves letting go of doubt, fear, and the need for external validation, and instead, learning to trust the inherent intelligence of our intuitive faculties. Cultivating self-awareness and discernment allows us to differentiate between genuine intuitive guidance and the noise of the ego or external influences.

CONCLUSION

Nurturing intuition and inner knowing is a transformative journey of self-discovery, empowerment, and alignment with the deeper truths of our being. By cultivating receptivity, attunement, and trust, we can awaken to the innate wisdom that resides within us and live more authentically and purposefully.

5

SPIRITUAL AND DREAM STATES

The journey of exploring consciousness, spanning from ordinary waking states to profound enlightenment and heightened dream awareness, is inherently intertwined with the notions of vibration and frequency. Much like every element in the universe resonates at its distinct frequency, consciousness also manifests in diverse levels of vibrational energy.

States of Consciousness to Enlightenment

The journey from ordinary states of consciousness to enlightenment is a profound exploration of the mind, heart, and spirit, encompassing various stages of awakening and realisation. Drawing from spiritual traditions, psychology, and neuroscience, we can delineate a path that illuminates the progression of consciousness towards enlightenment.

ORDINARY WAKING CONSCIOUSNESS: Ordinary waking consciousness represents the baseline state of awareness characterised by everyday experiences, thoughts, emotions, and perceptions. In this state, individuals are identified with the ego and the external world, often driven by desires, fears, and conditioned patterns of thinking.

EXPANDED STATES OF CONSCIOUSNESS: Expanded states of consciousness encompass experiences that transcend ordinary waking awareness, such as meditation, contemplation, and altered states of consciousness induced by psychedelics or deep spiritual practices. These states may involve heightened awareness, profound insights, and a sense of interconnectedness with all existence (Grof, 2006).

TRANSCENDENCE OF EGO IDENTITY: The journey towards enlightenment involves transcending the limitations of ego identity and recognising the impermanent nature of the self. Through self-inquiry, mindfulness, and spiritual practices, individuals cultivate awareness of the ego's illusory nature and awaken to the deeper essence of their being (Tolle, 2004).

AWAKENING TO PRESENCE AND STILLNESS: Awakening to presence and stillness involves recognising the timeless dimension of consciousness that exists beyond the incessant chatter of the mind. Through practices such as meditation and mindfulness, individuals learn to abide in the present moment, accessing a state of inner peace, clarity, and inner knowing (Kabat-Zinn, 1990).

. . .

UNITY CONSCIOUSNESS AND NON-DUALITY: Unity consciousness and non-duality represent the realisation of the interconnectedness of all existence and the dissolution of dualistic perceptions of self and other. In this state, individuals experience a profound sense of oneness with the universe, recognising that separation is an illusion and that all beings are expressions of the same divine consciousness (Wilber, 2000).

ENLIGHTENMENT AND SELF-REALISATION: Enlightenment is the culmination of the spiritual journey, representing the direct realisation of one's true nature as pure awareness or consciousness. In this state, the individual transcends the limitations of the ego-mind and abides in a state of unconditional love, compassion, and wisdom (Hanh, 2012).

CONCLUSION

The path from states of consciousness to enlightenment is a transformative journey of self-discovery, spiritual growth, and awakening to the deeper dimensions of existence. By cultivating awareness, presence, and inner wisdom, individuals can embark on a journey towards enlightenment and realise their fullest potential as spiritual beings.

The Stages of Spiritual Awakening and Their Impact on Consciousness

The journey of spiritual awakening is a transformative process that unfolds in stages, leading individuals from a state of unconsciousness to profound realisation and enlightenment. Drawing from spiritual traditions and contemporary insights, we can explore the stages of spiritual awakening and their profound effects on consciousness.

INITIAL AWAKENING: The initial stage of spiritual awakening often begins with a sense of discontent or inner questioning about the nature of reality and one's purpose in life. Individuals may experience a deep longing for something more meaningful or a shift in perception that opens them to new possibilities (Tolle, 2004).

SEEKING AND INQUIRY: During the seeking and inquiry stage, individuals actively pursue answers to existential questions and explore various spiritual teachings, practices, and modalities. This stage may involve reading spiritual literature, attending workshops, seeking guidance from teachers, and engaging in introspective practices such as meditation and self-inquiry (Hanh, 2012).

OPENING TO PRESENCE: The opening to presence stage involves a shift in consciousness towards greater awareness of the present moment. Individuals may experience moments of deep stillness, inner peace, and clarity as they become more attuned to the here and now. This stage marks the beginning of a deeper connection with the inner self and the underlying reality of existence (Kabat-Zinn, 1990).

EGO DISSOLUTION: Ego dissolution is a pivotal stage in the spiritual awakening process, characterised by the dismantling of egoic structures and identification with the false self. Individuals may experience intense periods of emotional upheaval, ego resistance, and existential crisis as they confront the illusion of separateness and surrender to the flow of life (Tolle, 2004).

TRANSCENDENCE AND UNITY CONSCIOUSNESS: Transcendence and unity consciousness represent the pinnacle of spiritual awakening, where individuals experience a profound sense of oneness with all existence. In this stage, the boundaries between self and other dissolve, and individuals recognise the interconnectedness of all beings and the underlying unity of consciousness (Wilber, 2000).

INTEGRATION AND EMBODIMENT: Integration and embodiment involve the integration of spiritual insights and realisations into everyday life. Individuals learn to embody the qualities of presence, compassion, and authenticity in their interactions with others and the world around them. This stage marks the beginning of a lifelong journey of self-discovery, growth, and service (Hanh, 2012).

CONCLUSION

The stages of spiritual awakening profoundly impact consciousness, leading to shifts in perception, identity, and relationship with the world. As individuals progress through these stages, they undergo profound transformations that awaken them to the deeper dimensions of existence and the inherent divinity within themselves.

Dream State of Consciousness and Utilising Dream Analysis

Dreams represent a fascinating aspect of human consciousness, providing insights into our innermost thoughts, emotions, and subconscious processes. Understanding the dream state of consciousness and learning how to analyse dreams can serve as a powerful tool for personal growth, self-discovery, and problem-solving in daily life.

THE NATURE OF DREAMS: Dreams occur during the rapid eye movement (REM) stage of sleep and involve a complex interplay of neural activity, memory consolidation, and emotional processing. During this time, the brain synthesises fragments of memory, experience, and emotion into a cohesive narrative that unfolds in the theatre of the mind.

WHILE DREAMS often contain surreal or fantastical elements, they also reflect underlying psychological themes, unresolved conflicts, and unconscious desires that influence our thoughts, emotions, and behaviours (Hobson, 2002).

ANALYSING DREAMS: Dream analysis involves the exploration and interpretation of the symbols, themes, and narratives that emerge during sleep. By examining the content and context of dreams, we can gain valuable insights into our inner psyche and

uncover hidden aspects of our personality, fears, and aspirations.

Carl Jung, a pioneering psychologist, introduced the concept
of archetypes and the collective unconscious, which underpin
the symbolic language of dreams. Jungian dream analysis
emphasises the importance of exploring recurring motifs, char-
acters, and symbols to unlock deeper layers of meaning and
insight (Jung, 1968).

Sigmund Freud, another influential figure in dream psychology, proposed that dreams serve as a pathway to the unconscious
mind, where repressed desires, fears, and conflicts manifest in
symbolic form. Freudian dream analysis focuses on uncovering
latent content beneath the manifest content of dreams, revealing
hidden motivations and unresolved issues (Freud, 1900).

UTILISING **Dream Analysis in Daily Life**: Dream analysis can
offer valuable guidance and assistance in various aspects of
daily life, including:

PROBLEM-SOLVING: Dreams often provide creative solutions,
alternative perspectives, and intuitive insights into real-life challenges and dilemmas. By reflecting on dream content and
extracting relevant themes or symbols, we can uncover innovative approaches to problem-solving and decision-making.

EMOTIONAL PROCESSING: Dreams serve as a safe space for
emotional processing and catharsis, allowing us to explore and
release pent-up emotions, anxieties, and fears. By acknowl-
edging and integrating the emotions that arise in dreams, we
can promote emotional healing and inner harmony.

. . .

SELF-DISCOVERY: Dream analysis fosters self-awareness and introspection, enabling us to explore our inner landscape, motivations, and aspirations. By paying attention to recurring dreams, symbols, and patterns, we can gain deeper insights into our psyche and cultivate greater self-understanding.

Practical Techniques for Dream Analysis:

Keep a dream journal: Recording dreams upon waking helps capture details and emotions that may fade with time. Reviewing dream journals allows for reflection and recognition of recurring themes and symbols.

REFLECT AND INTERPRET: Reflecting on dream content and exploring potential meanings through journaling, meditation, or dialogue with others can facilitate deeper understanding and insight.

SEEK GUIDANCE: Consulting with a therapist, dream analyst, or support group can provide additional perspectives and support in the process of dream analysis.

ANALYSING dreams can be a personal and subjective practice, but there are several resources available, including apps and books, that offer guidance and further techniques for interpreting dreams.

. . .

CONCLUSION

The dream state of consciousness offers a rich tapestry of symbolism, emotion, and insight that can enrich our understanding of ourselves and our lives. By embracing dream analysis as a tool for self-discovery and growth, we can tap into the wisdom of the unconscious mind and unlock the transformative potential of our dreams.

Dream Interpretation Across Cultures

Dream interpretation is a universal phenomenon that transcends cultural boundaries, yet the methods and symbolism used to decipher dreams vary widely across different cultures. Exploring dream interpretation practices across diverse cultural traditions provides insights into the richness of human consciousness and the symbolic language of the unconscious mind.

ANCIENT EGYPT: In ancient Egyptian culture, dreams held profound significance and were believed to be messages from the gods or divine realms. Dream interpretation was an integral part of religious and political life, with trained priests serving as interpreters. Hieroglyphs and symbols depicted in Egyptian art and literature often reflect the importance of dreams in guiding personal and collective destiny (Quirke, 1992).

ANCIENT GREECE AND ROME: In ancient Greek and Roman civilisations, dreams were viewed as omens and portents that foretold future events or provided guidance from the gods. Greek philosophers such as Aristotle and Plato explored the nature of dreams and their relationship to the subconscious mind. The practice of oneiromancy, or dream divination, was prevalent in ancient Greece and Rome, with individuals seeking guidance from dream interpreters (Nutton, 2004).

INDIGENOUS CULTURES: Indigenous cultures around the world have rich traditions of dream interpretation that reflect their spiritual beliefs and worldview. In many indigenous societies, dreams are seen as a means of communication with ancestral spirits, nature, and the unseen realms. Dreaming plays a central role in healing, vision quests, and rites of passage ceremonies, with elders serving as interpreters and guides (Tedlock, 1992).

ISLAMIC TRADITION: In Islamic culture, dreams are considered a means of divine communication and guidance. The Prophet Muhammad emphasised the importance of dreams as a source of revelation and insight. Islamic dream interpretation, known as ta'bir, involves analysing dream symbols and narratives in the context of Islamic teachings and scripture. Dream interpretation books such as "The Interpretation of Dreams" by Ibn Sirin are widely consulted by Muslims seeking guidance (Sirin, 1992).

CHINESE AND EAST ASIAN TRADITIONS: Dream interpretation holds significance in Chinese and East Asian cultures, where dreams are seen as reflections of the balance and harmony of the universe. Chinese dream interpretation draws upon the principles of Taoism, Confucianism, and Buddhism, emphasising the interconnectedness of heaven, earth, and humanity. Dream symbols such as animals, colours, and natural elements carry specific meanings in Chinese culture (Wu, 2005).

. . .

MODERN PSYCHOLOGY: In contemporary Western psychology, dream interpretation draws from Freudian and Jungian perspectives, as well as cognitive and neuroscientific approaches. Freud emphasised the role of dreams in revealing unconscious desires and conflicts, while Jung explored the symbolic language of dreams and the collective unconscious. Modern psychotherapy incorporates dream analysis as a tool for self-discovery, insight, and healing (Freud, 1900; Jung, 1968).

CONCLUSION

Dream interpretation reflects the diversity of human culture and the universal quest for meaning and understanding. By exploring dream symbolism and interpretation practices across different cultures, we gain a deeper appreciation for the symbolic language of the unconscious mind and the profound insights that dreams offer into the human experience.

Exploring the Metaphysical World Through the Dream State

Dreams have long been recognised as a gateway to the metaphysical realm, providing a window into dimensions of reality beyond the confines of ordinary waking consciousness. By delving into the dream state, individuals can embark on journeys of exploration, discovery, and transformation that transcend the boundaries of time, space, and physicality.

METAPHYSICAL DIMENSIONS OF DREAMS: Dreams offer access to metaphysical dimensions of reality that lie beyond the constraints of the physical world. In the dream state, consciousness is liberated from the limitations of the body and ego, allowing for direct experiences of higher realms, spiritual beings, and alternate realities.

THE METAPHYSICAL DIMENSIONS of dreams encompass a vast array of experiences, including encounters with spirit guides, visits to celestial realms, astral projection, and lucid dreaming. These experiences provide glimpses into the interconnectedness of all existence and the underlying fabric of the universe (LaBerge, 1985).

SYMBOLISM AND ARCHETYPES: Dreams often communicate through symbolism, archetypes, and mythic imagery that resonate with the deep layers of the psyche and the collective unconscious. Archetypal symbols such as the wise old man, the shadow, and the hero's journey serve as doorways to the metaphysical realm, offering insights into universal truths and spiritual principles (Jung, 1968).

BY DECIPHERING the symbolic language of dreams, individuals can unravel hidden meanings, messages, and guidance from the higher self, spirit guides, or the collective wisdom of humanity (Van de Castle, 1994).

ASTRAL TRAVEL AND OUT-OF-BODY EXPERIENCES: The dream state provides fertile ground for astral travel and out-of-body experiences (OBEs), in which consciousness separates from the physical body and explores non-physical dimensions of reality. During OBEs, individuals may traverse astral planes, visit other realms, or commune with spiritual beings and guides (Monroe, 1971).

THROUGH CONSCIOUS INTENTION AND PRACTICE, individuals can learn to induce and control astral travel experiences, facilitating direct encounters with the metaphysical world and expanding their understanding of the nature of reality (Bruce, 1999).

SPIRITUAL GUIDANCE AND INSIGHT: Dreams serve as a conduit for spiritual guidance, insight, and revelation, offering opportunities for profound transformation and awakening. Spiritual seekers often receive guidance, wisdom, and healing in dreams, as well as visions of future events, past lives, and karmic patterns (Taylor, 2001).

BY CULTIVATING RECEPTIVITY, trust, and attunement to the wisdom of the dream state, individuals can deepen their connection to the metaphysical realm and align with their soul's purpose and evolution.

INTEGRATION AND APPLICATION: Exploring the metaphysical world through the dream state requires openness, curiosity, and a willingness to suspend disbelief. By keeping dream journals, practicing lucid dreaming techniques, and engaging in meditation and visualisation exercises, individuals can enhance their dream recall, lucidity, and ability to navigate the metaphysical landscape.

. . .

INTEGRATING insights from dreams into daily life fosters greater alignment, authenticity, and spiritual growth, empowering individuals to embody the wisdom and guidance received from the metaphysical realm (Garfield, 1998).

CONCLUSION

The dream state serves as a portal to the metaphysical world, offering seekers a pathway to explore, discover, and awaken to the deeper mysteries of existence. By embracing dreams as sacred gifts and windows to the soul, individuals can embark on transformative journeys of self-discovery, healing, and spiritual evolution.

6

ENVIRONMENTAL AND INTERNAL INFLUENCES

The Shifting Magnetic North Pole: Implications for the Physical and Energetic Environment

The magnetic North Pole, a point in the Northern Hemisphere towards which the Earth's magnetic field lines converge, is not static but rather dynamic, constantly in motion. In recent years, scientists have observed an acceleration in the movement of the magnetic North Pole, raising questions about its potential impact on the physical and energetic environment. This section explores the phenomenon of the shifting magnetic North Pole and its implications.

THE SHIFTING MAGNETIC NORTH POLE: The Earth's magnetic field is generated by the movement of molten iron within its outer core, creating a complex and dynamic system of magnetic lines of force. The magnetic North Pole, the point at which these lines converge and dip vertically into the Earth, is not fixed but rather subject to gradual drift and movement (Mandea & Korte, 2012).

. . .

WHILE THE MAGNETIC North Pole has historically migrated at a rate of about 10 kilometres per year, recent observations indicate a significant acceleration in its movement, with the pole shifting towards Siberia at a rate of approximately 55 kilometres per year in recent decades (Finlay et al., 2016).

POTENTIAL IMPACTS **on Navigation and Technology**: The shifting magnetic North Pole has practical implications for navigation, cartography, and geolocation systems that rely on magnetic compasses and magnetic declination values. As the magnetic North Pole moves, it can affect the accuracy of compass readings, leading to errors in navigation and mapping (Macmillan et al., 2019).

IN ADDITION, the movement of the magnetic North Pole may necessitate periodic updates and recalibrations of magnetic models and navigation charts to ensure the reliability and accuracy of magnetic-based systems (Chulliat et al., 2019).

GEOMAGNETIC VARIATIONS AND SPACE WEATHER: The Earth's magnetic field plays a crucial role in shielding the planet from solar wind and cosmic radiation, creating a protective magnetosphere that extends into space. Variations in the Earth's magnetic field, including the movement of the magnetic North Pole, can influence the behaviour of charged particles in the ionosphere and magnetosphere (Laundal & Richmond, 2017).

. . .

CHANGES in the Earth's magnetic field, such as magnetic reversals or fluctuations, can potentially impact space weather phenomena such as geomagnetic storms, auroral activity, and disruptions to satellite communications and power grids (Horton et al., 2020).

ENERGETIC AND METAPHYSICAL CONSIDERATIONS: Beyond its physical implications, the shifting magnetic North Pole may also have energetic and metaphysical effects on the Earth's subtle energy systems and human consciousness. Some spiritual and metaphysical traditions associate the Earth's magnetic field with energetic ley lines, vortices, and meridians that influence the flow of subtle energy (Hartmann, 1989).

THE MOVEMENT of the magnetic North Pole could potentially disrupt or realign these energetic pathways, leading to shifts in the Earth's energy grid and affecting human experiences of intuition, geomancy, and spiritual connection (Becker & Hagens, 1981).

SCIENTIFIC MONITORING AND RESEARCH: Scientists and researchers monitor the movement of the magnetic North Pole using a network of geomagnetic observatories, satellites, and magnetic surveys. By tracking changes in the Earth's magnetic field, scientists can better understand the underlying processes driving magnetic pole drift and its potential implications for Earth systems and technology (Maus et al., 2010).

. . .

ONGOING RESEARCH INTO GEOMAGNETISM, paleomagnetism, and Earth's dynamo processes aims to deepen our understanding of the complex interactions between the Earth's magnetic field, geophysical processes, and the broader Earth system (Gubbins, 2011).

CONCLUSION

The shifting magnetic North Pole represents a dynamic and multifaceted phenomenon with implications for navigation, technology, space weather, and subtle energy systems. By studying and monitoring magnetic pole drift, scientists can gain valuable insights into Earth's magnetic field dynamics and their broader impacts on the physical and energetic environment.

The Influence of the Moon on Human Physiology and Energy

The moon, Earth's only natural satellite, has captivated human imagination for millennia. Beyond its ethereal beauty, the moon exerts a subtle yet profound influence on various aspects of human physiology, behaviour, and energetic states. This chapter explores the multifaceted relationship between the moon and humans, drawing insights from scientific research and metaphysical perspectives.

BIOLOGICAL RHYTHMS AND LUNAR PHASES: Scientific studies have revealed correlations between lunar phases and human biology, particularly in relation to sleep patterns, reproductive cycles, and mood fluctuations (Cajochen et al., 2013). Lunar cycles, particularly the full moon, have been associated with changes in sleep architecture, including alterations in sleep duration, latency, and quality (Cajochen et al., 2013; Palagini et al., 2013).

SOME RESEARCH SUGGESTS that lunar cycles may influence hormonal fluctuations, menstrual cycles, and fertility rates in humans, although the evidence remains inconclusive and requires further investigation (Köhnke, 2005; Cutler et al., 1987).

PSYCHOLOGICAL AND BEHAVIOURAL EFFECTS: The lunar cycle has long been associated with changes in human behaviour and emotional states, giving rise to the notion of "lunar lunacy" or the belief that the full moon can trigger heightened emotions, erratic behaviour, and increased hospital admissions (Rotton & Kelly, 1985). While empirical evidence for lunar effects on human behaviour is mixed, anecdotal reports and cultural beliefs persist across diverse societies and traditions (Liebreich, 2002).

PSYCHOLOGICAL STUDIES HAVE EXPLORED the phenomenon of "moonstruck" behaviour and its potential psychological mechanisms, including confirmation bias, cultural priming, and societal expectations (Vitale & Viglione, 2015). The psychological significance of lunar cycles underscores the interconnectedness of human consciousness and celestial phenomena.

ENERGETIC AND METAPHYSICAL PERSPECTIVES: In metaphysical and spiritual traditions, the moon is believed to exert subtle energetic influences on human consciousness and subtle energy systems. Lunar phases, particularly the full moon and new moon, are considered auspicious times for spiritual practices, rituals, and intention setting (Cunningham, 2002).

THE FULL MOON is often associated with heightened psychic sensitivity, intuition, and emotional release, while the new moon symbolises renewal, intentionality, and inner reflection (Teixeira et al., 2019). Practices such as moon meditation, lunar yoga, and moon ceremonies are used to harness lunar energies and align with natural cycles (Budilovsky & Adamson, 2000).

CULTURAL AND SYMBOLIC SIGNIFICANCE: Across cultures and civilisations, the moon holds symbolic significance as a celestial archetype representing femininity, intuition, and the subconscious mind. Lunar deities, myths, and folklore abound in human history, reflecting diverse interpretations of the moon's influence on human affairs (Burland, 1985).

FROM ANCIENT LUNAR calendars to modern astrology, humans have sought to decode the symbolic language of the moon and its impact on individual destinies, relationships, and life cycles (Greene, 1985). The moon's cyclical nature mirrors the rhythms of life, death, and rebirth, inviting contemplation on the cyclical nature of existence (Eisler, 1987).

SCIENTIFIC INQUIRY AND CULTURAL HERITAGE: While scientific inquiry has elucidated some of the physiological and psychological effects of lunar cycles on humans, much remains unknown about the intricacies of this complex relationship. Interdisciplinary research integrating biological, psychological, and cultural perspectives can deepen our understanding of the moon's influence on human physiology, behaviour, and consciousness (Foster, 2013).

By HONOURING the cultural heritage and symbolic significance of the moon while embracing empirical inquiry and critical inquiry, humans can cultivate a holistic understanding of their relationship with the cosmos and the interconnected web of life (Braun et al., 2008).

CONCLUSION

The moon's influence on human physiology and energy transcends scientific inquiry, encompassing psychological, metaphysical, and cultural dimensions. By exploring the interplay between lunar cycles and human experience, we gain insights into the mysteries of consciousness, the rhythms of nature, and the eternal dance of light and shadow in the cosmos.

Frequencies of the Natural World

The natural world is a symphony of vibrations and frequencies, each element resonating with its own unique signature. From the gentle hum of the wind to the rhythmic pulse of the ocean waves, the frequencies of nature shape the environment, influence living organisms, and resonate with the cosmos. This chapter delves into the frequencies of the natural world, exploring their diverse manifestations and profound implications.

. . .

ACOUSTIC FREQUENCIES: Sound waves permeate the natural world, carrying information, energy, and communication across vast landscapes. From the melodic chirping of birds to the thunderous roar of waterfalls, acoustic frequencies are integral to the ecological balance and biodiversity of ecosystems (Krause, 2012).

ETHNOMUSICOLOGICAL STUDIES HAVE DOCUMENTED the rich tapestry of natural sounds produced by animals, insects, and geological formations, revealing intricate patterns of rhythm, pitch, and timbre that reflect the interconnectedness of life (Schafer, 1977).

GEOLOGICAL AND SEISMIC FREQUENCIES: Beneath the Earth's surface, geological processes generate seismic waves and vibrations that reverberate through the planet's crust. Earthquakes, volcanic eruptions, and tectonic movements emit low-frequency vibrations that can be detected and analysed by seismographs and geophysical instruments (Lay et al., 2010).

THE STUDY OF INFRASOUND, or low-frequency sound waves below the threshold of human hearing, offers insights into natural phenomena such as atmospheric disturbances, ocean currents, and seismic activity, illuminating the dynamic interactions between Earth's spheres (Milton et al., 1998).

ELECTROMAGNETIC FREQUENCIES: Electromagnetic radiation encompasses a broad spectrum of frequencies, from radio waves and microwaves to visible light and gamma rays. Natural sources of electromagnetic radiation, including sunlight, cosmic radiation, and geomagnetic fields, play essential roles in photosynthesis, navigation, and biological rhythms (Fröhlich, 1980).

ANIMALS AND PLANTS have evolved sophisticated mechanisms for detecting and responding to electromagnetic cues, using magnetic fields for orientation, navigation, and migration across vast distances (Wiltschko & Wiltschko, 2005).

BIOLOGICAL AND BIOENERGETIC FREQUENCIES: Living organisms emit subtle bioenergetic fields and electromagnetic frequencies that regulate cellular processes, metabolic functions, and physiological responses. The human body, for example, generates bioelectrical signals through the nervous system, heart, and brain, producing measurable electromagnetic fields (Popp et al., 1988).

BIOELECTROMAGNETIC RESEARCH EXPLORES the interactions between living systems and electromagnetic fields, investigating the effects of electromagnetic pollution, electromagnetic therapy, and bioresonance on health and well-being (Blank & Goodman, 2009).

HARMONIC RESONANCE AND SYNCHRONY: At the heart of the natural world lies the principle of harmonic resonance, wherein frequencies interact and synchronise to create coherence and harmony. Oscillatory phenomena such as entrainment, coherence, and resonance manifest across diverse scales of existence, from the synchronised flashing of fireflies to the collective behaviour of flocks and schools (Strogatz, 2003).

. . .

THE CONCEPT of resonance underscores the interconnectedness of all life forms and the fundamental unity of nature, as frequencies converge and resonate in a cosmic dance of creation and dissolution (Lanza & Berman, 2009).

CONCLUSION

The frequencies of the natural world form a web of interconnected vibrations that animate the fabric of existence. By attuning ourselves to the subtle rhythms and harmonies of nature, we deepen our connection to the Earth, cultivate reverence for life, and awaken to the profound beauty and wisdom encoded in the symphony of creation.

Vibrations of the Natural World

The natural world is a symphony of vibrations, resonating with diverse frequencies that shape the fabric of existence. From the gentle rustle of leaves in the wind to the thunderous crash of ocean waves, vibrations permeate every aspect of nature, revealing the interconnectedness and dynamism of life. This chapter explores the profound significance of vibrations in the natural world, drawing insights from scientific research and spiritual traditions.

VIBRATIONS IN SOUND: Sound waves propagate through the air, water, and solid materials, carrying information, energy, and emotion across landscapes and ecosystems. In the natural world, sound vibrations serve myriad functions, from communication and navigation to mate attraction and predator detection (Tyack, 2000).

ETHNOMUSICOLOGICAL STUDIES HAVE DOCUMENTED the rich diversity of natural sounds produced by animals, insects, and geological formations, revealing complex patterns of rhythm, pitch, and timbre that reflect the ecological balance and biodiversity of ecosystems (Schafer, 1977).

VIBRATIONS IN MOTION: Movement is intrinsic to the natural world, as organisms and elements oscillate, undulate, and pulsate in rhythmic harmony with the Earth's cycles. From the swaying of trees in the breeze to the dance of celestial bodies in the night sky, motion generates vibrations that resonate with the rhythms of life (Daubenmire, 1956).

. . .

BIOMECHANICAL STUDIES HAVE ELUCIDATED the mechanisms of motion in living organisms, revealing the biomechanical principles underlying locomotion, flight, and aquatic propulsion (Vogel, 2003).

VIBRATIONS IN LIGHT: Light is a fundamental force in the natural world, illuminating landscapes, nourishing photosynthetic organisms, and guiding biological rhythms. The electromagnetic spectrum encompasses a broad range of frequencies, from infrared to ultraviolet, each carrying unique information and energy (Kumar & Fouad, 2016).

THE STUDY of bioluminescence in marine organisms, fireflies, and fungi illuminates the intricate interplay between light production, chemical reactions, and ecological interactions, highlighting the diversity and adaptability of life forms (Haddock et al., 2010).

VIBRATIONS IN ENERGY: Energy flows through ecosystems in a continuous exchange of vibrations, sustaining the web of life and driving metabolic processes. From the photosynthetic conversion of solar energy to the biochemical transformations within living cells, energy vibrations animate the biosphere and fuel the cycles of growth and decay (Nelson & Cox, 2005).

ECOLOGICAL STUDIES HAVE EXPLORED the flow of energy through food webs, nutrient cycles, and trophic interactions, revealing the intricate dynamics of energy exchange and transformation in terrestrial and aquatic ecosystems (Odum, 1971).

VIBRATIONS IN SPIRITUALITY: Spiritual traditions and indigenous cultures recognise the sacredness of vibrations in the natural world, honouring the interconnectedness of all beings and the divine resonance of creation. Rituals, ceremonies, and sacred sites are imbued with vibrational significance, serving as conduits for spiritual communion and healing (Abram, 1997).

PRACTICES SUCH AS CHANTING, drumming, and meditation harness the power of sound vibrations to induce altered states of consciousness, promote inner harmony, and attune individuals to the cosmic rhythms of existence (Halpern, 2014).

CONCLUSION

The vibrations of the natural world are a testament to the dynamic interplay of energy, motion, and consciousness in the cosmos. By attuning ourselves to the subtle frequencies of nature, we deepen our connection to the Earth, awaken to the inherent wisdom of the universe, and embrace the sacredness of all life.

The Vibrations of Animals: Their Impact on Human Emotional Well-being

Animals possess a unique and profound ability to influence human emotional well-being through the vibrations they emit. In this chapter, we explore the fascinating interplay between animals and humans, the vibrational frequencies they emit, and the transformative effects they have on emotional health and well-being.

THE CONNECTION **Between Animals and Humans:** Animals hold a special place in the hearts and minds of humans, serving as companions, teachers, and sources of comfort and joy. The bond between animals and humans transcends language and culture, rooted in a deep connection that spans millennia (Serpell, 2002). Whether as pets, therapy animals, or wildlife, animals have the remarkable ability to evoke powerful emotional responses and foster a sense of connection and belonging.

THE VIBRATIONAL FREQUENCIES OF ANIMALS: Animals emit subtle energetic vibrations that resonate with the human energy field, influencing emotional states, mood, and overall well-being (Beck, 2012). These vibrational frequencies are shaped by the unique characteristics, behaviours, and qualities of each species, from the gentle purring of a cat to the majestic presence of a horse or the playful antics of a dog.

EFFECTS ON HUMAN **Emotional Well-being**

- **Stress Reduction:** Interacting with animals has been shown to reduce stress levels and promote relaxation in humans. The calming presence of animals, combined with their soothing vibrations, can help alleviate anxiety, lower blood pressure, and induce feelings of peace and tranquility (Barker & Dawson, 1998).

- **Emotional Support:** Animals provide unconditional love and acceptance, serving as steadfast companions during times of joy, sorrow, and transition. The emotional bond between humans and animals fosters a sense of connection, empathy, and mutual understanding, which can enhance emotional resilience and promote healing (Fine, 2010).

- **Enhanced Mood and Happiness:** Spending time with animals has been linked to improved mood, increased levels of happiness, and a greater sense of emotional well-being. The playful and affectionate nature of animals elicits laughter, joy, and a sense of lightness, lifting spirits and fostering a positive outlook on life (McNicholas & Collis, 2000).

Cultivating Relationships with Animals

Pet Ownership: Bringing animals into our homes as pets allows for daily interaction and companionship, fostering deep bonds and emotional connections. Whether caring for a cat, dog, bird, or fish, the presence of animals enriches our lives and brings joy and fulfilment.

Animal-Assisted Therapy: Animal-assisted therapy programs utilise the healing power of animals to support individuals with physical, emotional, and cognitive challenges. Therapy animals, such as dogs, horses, and dolphins, provide comfort, companionship, and motivation for individuals undergoing therapy and rehabilitation (Fine, 2015).

Nature Connection: Connecting with animals in their natural habitats, such as wildlife sanctuaries, zoos, and nature reserves, allows for a deeper appreciation of the beauty and diversity of the animal kingdom. Observing animals in their natural environment can inspire awe, wonder, and a sense of reverence for the interconnectedness of all living beings.

Conclusion

The vibrations emitted by animals have a profound impact on human emotional well-being, fostering connection, healing, and joy. By cultivating relationships with animals, whether as pets, therapy animals, or wildlife, humans can tap into the transformative power of the animal kingdom and enrich their lives in meaningful ways.

The Frequencies Emitted by Plants: Exploring Nature's Vibrational Symphony

Plants, the silent guardians of the natural world, emit subtle frequencies that contribute to the intricate tapestry of life on Earth. In this section, we delve into the fascinating realm of plant frequencies, exploring their vibrational signatures, the mechanisms behind their emission, and the profound impact they have on ecosystems and human well-being.

UNDERSTANDING Plant Frequencies

Plants, despite their outwardly serene appearance, are dynamic entities that communicate, interact, and respond to their environment through a myriad of biochemical and biophysical processes (Gagliano, 2014). At the heart of plant communication lies the emission of subtle frequencies that

encode information about their physiological state, environmental conditions, and interactions with other organisms.

Mechanisms of Frequency Emission

Bioelectrical Signalling: Plants generate electrical signals
through the movement of ions across cellular membranes, a
process known as action potential. These bioelectrical signals
propagate through the plant's tissues, coordinating growth,
development, and responses to environmental stimuli (Fromm
& Lautner, 2007).

Acoustic Emissions: Recent research has revealed that plants
also emit acoustic vibrations, albeit at frequencies beyond the
range of human hearing. These ultrasonic vibrations are generated by various physiological processes, such as transpiration,
photosynthesis, and stomatal movement (Gagliano et al., 2017).

Chemical Signalling: Plants release volatile organic compounds
(VOCs) into the atmosphere as part of their chemical signalling
repertoire. These VOCs serve as airborne messengers, communicating with neighbouring plants, beneficial microbes, and
pollinators, and defending against herbivores and pathogens
(Dicke & Baldwin, 2010).

IMPACT ON ECOSYSTEM Dynamics

Plant-Plant Communication: Through the emission of frequencies and chemical signals, plants engage in complex communication networks that facilitate cooperation, competition, and mutualistic interactions within ecosystems (Karban, 2008). Plants can detect and respond to cues from neighbouring individuals, adjusting their growth, physiology, and defence strategies accordingly.

Interactions with Other Organisms: Plant frequencies play a crucial role in mediating interactions with other organisms, including insects, birds, mammals, and microbes. For example, certain plants emit frequencies that attract pollinators or repel herbivores, shaping community structure and dynamics (Mäntylä et al., 2008).

IMPLICATIONS FOR HUMAN Well-being

Biophilia and Nature Connection: Exposure to natural environments rich in plant frequencies has been shown to enhance human well-being, reduce stress levels, and promote feelings of calmness and vitality (Bratman et al., 2012). The restorative effects of nature can be attributed, in part, to the subtle vibrations emitted by plants that resonate with the human energy field.

Aromatherapy and Herbal Medicine: Aromatherapy and herbal medicine harness the therapeutic properties of plant-derived compounds, including essential oils, phytochemicals, and floral essences. The subtle frequencies contained within these natural remedies interact with the body's energy systems, promoting balance, harmony, and holistic healing (Lawless, 2001).

Conclusion

The frequencies emitted by plants constitute a hidden dimension of the natural world, shaping ecosystems, mediating ecological interactions, and enriching human experiences. By deepening our understanding of plant frequencies and their implications for life on Earth, we gain a deeper appreciation for the interconnectedness of all living beings and the vibrational symphony that sustains our planet.

Exploring the Frequency & Vibration of Emotions

Emotions are complex, dynamic experiences that play a fundamental role in shaping human consciousness and behaviour. In this chapter, we delve into the intriguing realm of emotions, exploring their vibrations, frequencies, and the profound impact they have on the human energy field.

UNDERSTANDING EMOTIONS: Emotions are multidimensional states characterised by subjective feelings, physiological responses, cognitive appraisals, and behavioural expressions (Levenson, 1994). They encompass a wide range of experiences, from joy and love to sadness, anger, fear, and beyond.

EMOTIONS SERVE AS POWERFUL MESSENGERS, conveying important information about our internal state, desires, needs, and relationships with others (Ekman, 1992). They influence perception, decision-making, and interpersonal interactions, shaping the quality of our lives and relationships.

THE VIBRATIONAL NATURE OF EMOTIONS: From a metaphysical perspective, emotions are believed to possess vibrational frequencies that resonate with the human energy field (Hunt, 1995). Each emotion carries its own unique energetic signature, which can be perceived and felt by sensitive individuals.

HIGH-VIBRATIONAL EMOTIONS SUCH AS LOVE, joy, gratitude, and compassion are associated with feelings of expansion, lightness, and connection to the higher self or divine consciousness (Hicks & Hicks, 2004). These emotions uplift the spirit, enhance well-being, and promote harmony in relationships and communities.

CONVERSELY, low-vibrational emotions such as fear, anger, resentment, and shame are characterised by feelings of contraction, heaviness, and disconnection from the self and others (Hicks & Hicks, 2004). These emotions can drain energy, disrupt balance, and contribute to physical, emotional, and spiritual distress.

IMPACT **on the Human Energy Field:** Emotions exert a profound influence on the human energy field, also known as the aura or biofield (Brennan, 1987). High-vibrational emotions expand and elevate the energy field, whereas low-vibrational emotions contract and distort its natural radiance and coherence.

. . .

RESEARCH in the field of energy medicine suggests that emotions can be "felt" in the energy field as subtle sensations, vibrations, or disturbances (Brennan, 1993). Prolonged or intense emotional states can create energetic imbalances, blockages, or disturbances that impact physical health, mental clarity, and emotional well-being.

CULTIVATING EMOTIONAL AWARENESS AND RESILIENCE: Developing emotional awareness and resilience is essential for navigating the rich tapestry of human emotions and maintaining energetic balance (Goleman, 1995). Mindfulness practices, meditation, and somatic awareness techniques can help individuals become more attuned to their emotions, discerning their vibrational qualities and effects on the energy field.

CULTIVATING A PRACTICE OF EMOTIONAL SELF-REGULATION, self-compassion, and conscious choice-making empowers individuals to consciously work with their emotions, transforming lower-vibrational states into higher-vibrational ones (Davidson et al., 2003). This process fosters emotional intelligence, spiritual growth, and holistic well-being.

CONCLUSION

Emotions are dynamic phenomena that permeate the fabric of human experience, influencing consciousness, perception, and reality itself. By understanding the vibrational nature of emotions and cultivating emotional awareness and resilience, individuals can harness the transformative power of emotions to create lives of greater joy, fulfilment, and alignment with the divine.

7

HEALING AND WELLBEING

Promoting Peace through Frequencies and Vibrations

The concept of promoting peace through frequencies and vibrations taps into the profound understanding that everything in the universe is in a state of vibration, resonating with its own unique frequency. This chapter explores how frequencies and vibrations can serve as powerful tools for fostering peace and harmony, drawing insights from scientific research, spiritual traditions, and holistic practices.

RESONANCE AND HARMONY: Resonance is where two oscillating systems synchronise their vibrations when their frequencies align (Strogatz, 2003). This synchronisation to harmonious frequencies allows individuals and communities to establish coherence, fostering interconnectedness and unity (McCraty et al., 2003).

. . .

SOUND HEALING PRACTICES, including chanting, toning, and mantra recitation, harness resonant frequencies to induce relaxation, balance, and inner peace (Goleman & Schwartz, 1976). When two vibrating entities are in proximity, the physics of their interaction involve the transfer of energy from the stronger vibration to the weaker one through resonance.

THIS PHENOMENON, governed by classical mechanics and wave theory, occurs as waves propagate through the shared medium. When frequencies align, energy transfer between the entities amplifies the vibration of the weaker entity.

THE SCIENCE OF SOUND and Vibration: Scientific research in the field of psychoacoustics has revealed the profound effects of sound and vibration on human physiology, psychology, and consciousness (Särkämö et al., 2013). Sound frequencies can modulate brainwave activity, alter neurotransmitter levels, and promote emotional well-being, offering therapeutic benefits for stress reduction, anxiety management, and trauma healing (Lehrer et al., 2010).

STUDIES on the impact of music therapy, binaural beats, and harmonic resonance have shown promising results in alleviating symptoms of post-traumatic stress disorder (PTSD), depression, and chronic pain, highlighting the potential of sound-based interventions for promoting mental health and emotional resilience (van der Kolk, 2014).

.   .   .

THE HUMAN AUDITORY system can perceive a wide range of frequencies, typically ranging from 20 Hz to 20,000 Hz (hertz). However, even frequencies beyond the audible range, known as infrasound and ultrasound, can still impact the body. Infrasound, below the threshold of human hearing, has been associated with feelings of unease, fear, and discomfort (Leventhall, 2007). Ultrasound, on the other hand, while also inaudible, has been explored for its potential therapeutic effects, such as tissue regeneration and pain relief (Hasegawa et al., 2019).

THESE FINDINGS UNDERSCORE the multifaceted role of sound and vibration in influencing human well-being and highlight the importance of further research in harnessing their therapeutic potential.

SPIRITUAL AND METAPHYSICAL PERSPECTIVES: Spiritual traditions and indigenous cultures have long recognised the transformative power of sound and vibration for healing, purification, and spiritual awakening (Halpern, 2014). Sacred chants, hymns, and mantras are used in religious rituals and ceremonies to invoke divine presence, cultivate inner peace, and elevate consciousness (Gardner, 1990).

THE CONCEPT OF NADA BRAHMA, or "sound is God," underscores the belief that the universe is comprised of vibrational energy, and that the divine essence resonates within all beings and phenomena (Kakar, 1989).

. . .

GLOBAL SOUNDSCAPES AND SONIC SANCTUARIES: In an increasingly interconnected world, the preservation of natural and cultural soundscapes is essential for promoting peace and environmental stewardship (Krause, 2012). Sound ecologists advocate for the protection of biodiversity hotspots, acoustic sanctuaries, and quiet zones where the natural symphony of life can flourish (Krause & Rabinowitz, 2019).

INITIATIVES such as the World Listening Project and the Quiet Parks International aim to raise awareness about the importance of acoustic ecology and the need to mitigate noise pollution in urban, rural, and marine environments (Schafer, 1977).

COMMUNITY RESONANCE AND SOCIAL HARMONY: Sound-based practices, including group chanting, drum circles, and singing circles, can foster a sense of community resonance and social cohesion, transcending cultural barriers and promoting cross-cultural understanding (Trehub, 2001). Participatory music-making activities enable individuals to express their creativity, celebrate diversity, and forge meaningful connections with others (Cross, 2014).

COLLABORATIVE SOUND PROJECTS, such as community choirs, orchestras, and street performances, serve as platforms for collective expression, collective healing, and collective action, inspiring positive social change and grassroots activism (Perkins, 2001).

CONCLUSION

The promotion of peace through frequencies and vibrations represents a holistic approach to healing and transformation, integrating scientific inquiry, spiritual wisdom, and community engagement. By harnessing the power of sound and vibration, individuals and societies can cultivate inner harmony, restore balance to the Earth, and co-create a world of peace and compassion.

The Transformative Effects of Meditation on Consciousness

Meditation, an ancient practice with roots in various spiritual traditions, offers profound insights into the nature of consciousness and the human experience. In this chapter, we explore the effects of meditation on consciousness and delve into various techniques that facilitate inner exploration, self-discovery, and spiritual growth.

MEDITATION AND CONSCIOUSNESS: Meditation is a contemplative practice that involves focusing attention, cultivating mindfulness, and achieving a state of inner stillness and presence. It provides a pathway to explore the depths of consciousness, expand awareness, and transcend the limitations of the egoic mind (Lutz et al., 2008).

CONSCIOUSNESS, the essence of awareness and experience, encompasses the totality of human perception, cognition, and subjective reality. Meditation offers a direct experiential encounter with consciousness, allowing individuals to explore the nature of self, reality, and existence (Tang et al., 2015).

. . .

EFFECTS OF MEDITATION ON CONSCIOUSNESS: Scientific research has demonstrated that meditation can induce profound changes in brain structure and function, leading to enhanced cognitive function, emotional regulation, and overall well-being (Hölzel et al., 2011).

LONG-TERM MEDITATION PRACTICE has been associated with increased grey matter density in brain regions involved in attention, memory, and emotional processing. These structural changes reflect the plasticity and adaptability of the human brain in response to contemplative practices (Fox et al., 2014).

TECHNIQUES OF MEDITATION

There are numerous techniques of meditation, each offering a unique approach to cultivating mindfulness, concentration, and insight. Some of the most common meditation practices include:

- **Mindfulness meditation:** Involves observing the present moment with non-judgmental awareness, focusing attention on breath, sensations, or thoughts (Kabat-Zinn, 2003).

- **Loving-kindness meditation (Metta):** Cultivates feelings of compassion, empathy, and goodwill towards oneself and others, fostering emotional resilience and interpersonal connection (Salzberg, 1995).

- **Transcendental meditation (TM):** Involves silently repeating a mantra, a specific sound or phrase, to quiet the mind and access deeper states of consciousness (Orme-Johnson et al., 2010).

- **Vipassana meditation:** Involves insight meditation, observing the impermanent nature of sensations, thoughts, and emotions, and cultivating equanimity and wisdom (Goldstein & Kornfield, 2002).

INTEGRATION AND APPLICATION: Meditation is not just a solitary practice but a way of life that can permeate every aspect of one's existence. By integrating mindfulness, compassion, and presence into daily activities, individuals can cultivate greater clarity, authenticity, and inner peace (Siegel, 2010).

MEDITATION IS ALSO BEING INTEGRATED into various therapeutic approaches, educational settings, and corporate environments as a means of reducing stress, enhancing resilience, and fostering emotional intelligence (Hassed et al., 2015).

CONCLUSION

Meditation serves as a gateway to the exploration of consciousness and the realisation of our true nature. Through dedicated practice and inner exploration, individuals can awaken to the timeless wisdom that lies within and cultivate a deeper sense of connection, purpose, and fulfilment.

Vibrational Healing

Vibrational healing is a holistic approach to wellness that recognises the interconnectedness of body, mind, and spirit, and harnesses the transformative power of vibrational frequencies to promote health, balance, and vitality. In this chapter, we delve into the principles and practices of vibrational healing, examining its foundations, techniques, and therapeutic applications.

UNDERSTANDING Vibrational Medicine

Vibrational medicine is based on the premise that everything in the universe is in a state of vibration, resonating with its own unique frequency. From subatomic particles to celestial bodies, all matter and energy exhibit vibrational qualities that influence health and well-being (Gerber, 2001).

IN VIBRATIONAL HEALING, illness and imbalance are viewed as disruptions in the body's energetic field, resulting from stress, trauma, and negative emotions. By restoring harmony and coherence to the energy system, vibrational therapies aim to facilitate self-healing and restore optimal functioning (Tiller, 1997).

MODALITIES OF VIBRATIONAL Healing

Vibrational healing encompasses a diverse array of modalities, including sound therapy, energy medicine, flower essences, and crystal healing. Each modality utilises specific frequencies and vibrations to induce states of relaxation, balance, and alignment (Hoffmann, 2003).

· · ·

SOUND THERAPY EMPLOYS instruments such as tuning forks, singing bowls, and gongs to produce harmonious vibrations that resonate with the body's cells, tissues, and organs. The entrainment of brainwave patterns and the release of endorphins contribute to the therapeutic effects of sound healing (Gerber, 2001).

ENERGY MEDICINE MODALITIES, such as Reiki, Qi Gong, and Healing Touch, work with the body's subtle energy fields to remove blockages, restore flow, and promote energetic balance. Practitioners channel healing energy through the hands, directing it to areas of need and facilitating the body's innate healing intelligence (Eden, 2008).

FLOWER ESSENCES, derived from the vibrational imprint of flowers, plants, and gemstones, address emotional and spiritual imbalances by harmonising the subtle energies of the psyche. Bach flower remedies, for example, support emotional well-being and promote inner harmony by addressing negative thought patterns and emotional states (Kaminski & Katz, 2000).

THE SCIENCE of Vibrational Healing

Vibrational healing encompasses a diverse array of practices that harness the power of vibrational frequencies to promote physical and emotional well-being.

- **Ultrasound Therapy:** Utilising high-frequency sound waves to penetrate tissues and stimulate cellular activity, ultrasound therapy has been shown to enhance tissue repair and alleviate pain (Lubart et al., 2005).

- **Sound Therapy:** Involving the therapeutic use of sound frequencies to induce relaxation and reduce stress, sound therapy has demonstrated benefits for mental health and emotional well-being (Gerber, 2001).

- **Biofield Therapies:** Practices such as Reiki and therapeutic touch work with the body's energy fields to promote balance and harmony, potentially enhancing overall health (Baldwin et al., 2013).

- **Mind-Body Interventions:** Including meditation, yoga, and mindfulness practices, these interventions leverage the connection between the mind and body to promote healing and alleviate symptoms of various conditions (Black et al., 2013).

QUANTUM PHYSICS OFFERS a theoretical framework for understanding the principles of vibrational healing, suggesting that consciousness, intention, and resonance play fundamental roles in shaping the nature of reality (Dossey, 2009).

TOGETHER, these practices offer holistic approaches to health and wellness, addressing the interconnectedness of mind, body, and spirit.

· · ·

INTEGRATION AND HOLISTIC WELLNESS: Vibrational healing complements conventional medical approaches by addressing the multidimensional nature of health and illness. Integrative healthcare models incorporate vibrational therapies alongside conventional treatments, emphasising the importance of personalised care, patient empowerment, and holistic wellness (Astin et al., 2003).

As INTEREST in complementary and alternative medicine continues to grow, vibrational healing modalities are gaining recognition as effective tools for promoting self-care, resilience, and spiritual growth. By honouring the interconnectedness of body, mind, and spirit, vibrational healing invites individuals to embark on a journey of self-discovery and transformation (Gerber, 2001).

CONCLUSION

Vibrational healing offers a profound pathway to health and wholeness, inviting individuals to explore the depths of their inner landscape and awaken to the innate wisdom of the body-mind-spirit connection. By harmonising with the natural rhythms and frequencies of the universe, vibrational therapies empower individuals to reclaim their vitality.

Healing Through Sound Therapy: The Power of Gong, Crystal Bowls, and Tibetan Bowls

Sound therapy, an ancient healing modality, harnesses the transformative power of vibrations and frequencies to restore balance, promote wellness, and facilitate spiritual growth. In this chapter, we explore the profound effects of sound therapy, focusing on the therapeutic properties of the gong, crystal bowls, and Tibetan bowls, and examining their resonance with natural frequencies and vibrations.

THE GONG: **An Ancient Instrument of Healing**: The gong, an ancient and revered instrument in Asian cultures, emits resonant tones that deeply penetrate the body, mind, and spirit (Hess, 2016). Its rich spectrum of harmonics and overtones creates a sonic bath of vibrations, used historically in rituals, ceremonies, and healing practices across cultures.

THESE VIBRATIONS INDUCE profound states of relaxation, meditation, and altered consciousness, supported by research in sound therapy and vibrational healing (Wang et al., 2017). Gong meditation sessions are known to alleviate stress, anxiety, and promote overall well-being. Additionally, the gong's resonance synchronises brainwave patterns, enhancing mental clarity and spiritual connection (Chang et al., 2019).

PRACTITIONERS UTILISE GONG baths or immersion experiences to induce deep relaxation, meditation, and introspection, facilitating emotional release, energetic clearing, and spiritual awakening (Collins, 2011).

CRYSTAL SINGING BOWLS: **Emissaries of Pure Tone**: Crystal singing bowls, crafted from pure quartz crystal, emit crystalline tones and frequencies that resonate with the body's energy centres, or chakras. Each bowl corresponds to a specific chakra, emitting harmonics and overtones that balance and align the subtle energy system (Goldman, 2003).

THE CRYSTALLINE PURITY of quartz imbues crystal singing bowls with a unique clarity and potency, amplifying intentions, prayers, and healing intentions. Sound healers and therapists incorporate crystal bowls into meditation, yoga, and energy healing sessions to promote relaxation, stress reduction, and spiritual attunement (Goldman, 2011).

TIBETAN SINGING BOWLS: **Portals to Inner Stillness:** Tibetan singing bowls, ancient instruments of Himalayan wisdom, produce resonant vibrations that evoke a sense of inner calm, tranquility, and serenity. Crafted from a blend of metals, each bowl emits a unique set of frequencies and harmonics that soothe the nervous system and induce states of deep meditation (Jansen, 2017).

SOUND BATHS with Tibetan singing bowls offer participants an opportunity to journey inward, exploring the depths of consciousness and accessing states of expanded awareness. The bowls' subtle vibrations dissolve energetic blockages, awaken dormant potentials, and facilitate holistic healing (Wiedemann, 2013).

RESONANCE **with Natural Frequencies and Vibrations:** While scientific research has yet to conclusively establish a direct correlation between specific frequencies of gongs, crystal bowls, and

Tibetan bowls and natural resonances, anecdotal evidence and experiential accounts suggest that these instruments resonate with the subtle energies of the Earth and cosmos (Chang et al., 2014).

SOME PROPONENTS of sound therapy propose that gongs, crystal bowls, and Tibetan bowls may harmonise with the Earth's Schumann Resonance, a natural electromagnetic frequency range that resonates with human brainwaves and biorhythms (Polk, 1982).

INTEGRATION AND TRANSFORMATION: As sound therapy continues to gain recognition as a complementary healing modality, practitioners and researchers are exploring innovative applications and techniques for integrating gongs, crystal bowls, and Tibetan bowls into clinical settings, wellness centres, and holistic practices (Hammer, 2012).

THROUGH ONGOING EXPLORATION AND COLLABORATION, sound healers, therapists, and musicians are co-creating a vibrant tapestry of sonic medicine, offering pathways to healing, transformation, and self-discovery for individuals and communities worldwide (Halpern, 2014).

CONCLUSION

The healing power of sound therapy, exemplified by the gong, crystal bowls, and Tibetan bowls, transcends cultural boundaries and historical epochs, offering a timeless invitation to explore the depths of consciousness and the mysteries of the universe.

The Energetic Vibrations of Aromatherapy

Aromatherapy, the therapeutic use of essential oils derived from plants, has been practiced for centuries for its ability to promote physical, emotional, and spiritual well-being. In this chapter, we explore the fascinating question of whether aromatherapy possesses an energy vibration or frequency that influences the human energy field.

UNDERSTANDING AROMATHERAPY: Aromatherapy is based on the premise that aromatic compounds found in essential oils contain potent therapeutic properties that can affect the body, mind, and spirit (Buckle, 2003). These volatile plant extracts are obtained through distillation or cold-pressing methods and retain the natural essence and energy of the plant from which they are derived.

ENERGETIC PROPERTIES OF ESSENTIAL OILS: Essential oils are believed to possess subtle energetic qualities that resonate with the human energy field, or aura (Price, 1999). Each essential oil is composed of various chemical constituents that contribute to its unique aroma, therapeutic effects, and energetic signature.

THE CONCEPT of vibrational medicine suggests that essential oils emit specific frequencies or vibrations that can harmonise and balance the body's energy centres, or chakras, promoting health and vitality (Gerber, 2001). These vibrations are thought to interact with the subtle energy pathways of the body, such as meridians in Traditional Chinese Medicine (Tisserand & Young, 2014).

. . .

SCIENTIFIC PERSPECTIVES: While the concept of energy vibrations in aromatherapy is primarily rooted in holistic and esoteric traditions, there is growing interest in exploring the scientific basis of these claims (Battista & Tattelman, 2017). Some researchers propose that the aromatic molecules in essential oils may interact with the olfactory system and limbic system of the brain, influencing mood, emotions, and physiological responses (Buchbauer, 1993).

QUANTUM PHYSICS also suggests that everything in the universe, including essential oils, vibrates at its own unique frequency (Gerber, 2001). While more research is needed to fully understand the energetic properties of essential oils, anecdotal evidence and experiential observations support their therapeutic efficacy and subtle energetic effects.

APPLICATION AND EXPERIENCE: Practitioners of aromatherapy often incorporate the concept of energetic vibrations into their practice, selecting essential oils based on their specific energetic qualities and therapeutic benefits (Price, 1999). For example, lavender oil is renowned for its calming and balancing effects, while peppermint oil is invigorating and uplifting.

INDIVIDUALS MAY EXPERIENCE the subtle energetic effects of aromatherapy through inhalation, topical application, or diffusion of essential oils in the environment. The aromatic molecules interact with the body's energy field, promoting relaxation, stress relief, emotional release, and energetic alignment (Tisserand & Young, 2014).

CONCLUSION

While the concept of energetic vibrations in aromatherapy may be difficult to quantify scientifically, it holds profound significance in holistic healing traditions and experiential practices. By exploring the subtle energetic qualities of essential oils and integrating them into daily self-care rituals, individuals can enhance their overall well-being and connect more deeply with the healing power of nature.

Crystal Energy: Vibrations, Healing Benefits, and Activation Techniques

Crystals have long captivated human imagination with their dazzling beauty and metaphysical properties. In this chapter, we explore the profound world of crystal energy, vibrations, healing benefits, and the essential techniques for activating and cleansing crystals.

CRYSTAL ENERGY AND VIBRATIONS: Crystals are endowed with a unique energy signature that resonates with the Earth's electromagnetic field and cosmic forces. This energy emanates from the crystalline lattice structure of minerals, which imparts distinct vibrational frequencies to each crystal (Simmons & Ahsian, 2007).

WHEN A CRYSTAL IS SUBJECTED to external stimuli or intention, it vibrates at its inherent frequency, emitting subtle energies that interact with the human energy field, or aura. This resonance facilitates energetic balance, emotional healing, and spiritual transformation (Hall, 2011).

HEALING BENEFITS OF CRYSTALS: Crystals are believed to cleanse energy by absorbing, transmuting, and releasing stagnant or negative energies from their surroundings (Gienger, 2013). Proponents of crystal healing suggest that crystals have the ability to resonate at specific frequencies and interact with the body's subtle energy systems, helping to restore balance and harmony (Hall, 2009).

CRYSTALS POSSESS a wide array of healing properties that are attributed to their unique composition, colour, and energetic qualities. For example, amethyst is known for its calming and purifying effects, while rose quartz promotes love and compassion (Gienger, 2013).

CRYSTAL HEALING THERAPIES involve placing crystals on or around the body to absorb, amplify, and transmit healing energies. This process helps to clear energetic blockages, activate chakras, and restore equilibrium to the subtle energy system (Lilly, 2019).

ACTIVATING CRYSTALS: Activating crystals is the process of attuning them to their optimal vibrational frequency and aligning them with your intentions or healing goals. This can be achieved through various methods, such as intention setting, visualisation, and programming (Simmons, 2005).

. . .

To activate a crystal, hold it in your hands, close your eyes, and focus your intention on infusing the crystal with your desired energy or purpose. Visualise white light surrounding the crystal and see it radiating with vibrancy and vitality (Hall, 2011).

Cleansing Crystals: Cleansing crystals is essential for removing energetic imprints, negative vibrations, and residual energies that may accumulate over time. Crystals can absorb energies from their environment and previous interactions, which can diminish their effectiveness (Eason, 2015).

There are several methods for cleansing crystals, including smudging with sage or palo santo, bathing in saltwater, sunlight or moonlight, and using sound vibrations from singing bowls or tuning forks (Gienger, 2013).As a general rule of thumb (with some exceptions), crystals ending with "ite" tend to dissolve in water.

Hold the crystal under running water, visualise the impurities being washed away, and set the intention for the crystal to be purified and revitalised. Alternatively, place the crystal in a bowl of saltwater or bury it in the earth for a few hours to absorb negative energies (Lilly, 2019).

Conclusion

Harnessing the energy of crystals offers a powerful pathway to holistic healing, self-discovery, and spiritual growth. By understanding the vibrational properties of crystals, exploring their healing benefits, and practicing activation and cleansing techniques, individuals can cultivate a deeper connection to the natural world and unlock the transformative potential of these precious gems.

Enhancing Health and Well-being with Ayurveda

Ayurveda, the ancient Indian system of medicine, offers holistic approaches to promote health and well-being by balancing the body, mind, and spirit. Rooted in natural principles and tailored to individual constitutions, Ayurvedic practices encompass various modalities that address physical, mental, and emotional aspects of health. Drawing from centuries of wisdom, Ayurveda provides numerous ways to optimise well-being and vitality.

DIETARY AND LIFESTYLE RECOMMENDATIONS: Ayurveda emphasises the importance of dietary choices and lifestyle habits in maintaining health. Recommendations are personalised based on an individual's unique constitution (dosha) to balance energies and promote harmony within the body. These may include consuming nourishing foods according to one's doshic type, practicing mindful eating, and following daily routines (dinacharya) that align with natural rhythms.

HERBAL REMEDIES AND MEDICINAL PLANTS: Ayurveda harnesses the healing power of herbs and medicinal plants to address various health concerns and imbalances. Herbal remedies are tailored to individual needs and may include formulations to support digestion, strengthen immunity, and promote overall well-being. Common Ayurvedic herbs such as ashwagandha, turmeric, and triphala are renowned for their therapeutic properties and extensive use in traditional healing practices.

YOGA AND PRANAYAMA: Yoga and pranayama (breath work) are integral components of Ayurvedic wellness practices that promote physical strength, flexibility, and mental clarity. Through asana (postures) and pranayama techniques, individuals can cultivate balance, release tension, and enhance vitality. These practices also facilitate the free flow of prana (life force energy) throughout the body, supporting overall health and rejuvenation.

PANCHAKARMA DETOXIFICATION: Panchakarma, a cornerstone of Ayurvedic therapy, involves comprehensive detoxification and rejuvenation treatments to purify the body and restore equilibrium. This holistic approach includes therapies such as massage (abhyanga), herbal steam therapy (swedana), and therapeutic enemas (basti) to eliminate toxins, strengthen tissues, and promote vitality at the cellular level.

MIND-BODY PRACTICES: Ayurveda recognises the inseparable connection between the mind and body, offering practices to foster emotional balance and mental well-being. Techniques such as meditation, mindfulness, and mantra recitation cultivate inner peace, reduce stress, and enhance mental clarity. Ayurvedic psychology also explores the role of emotions in health and provides tools for emotional healing and self-awareness.

. . .

CONCLUSION

Ayurveda offers a comprehensive framework for optimising health and well-being by integrating traditional wisdom with modern lifestyle practices. By embracing Ayurvedic principles and incorporating its holistic approaches into daily life, individuals can cultivate vitality, resilience, and inner harmony for long-lasting health and wellness.

Harnessing Energy for Personal Protection and Preservation

In a world filled with diverse energies, protecting one's own energy field is crucial for maintaining emotional balance, mental clarity, and spiritual well-being. In this chapter, we explore how individuals can use energy to safeguard and preserve their inner vitality, drawing from various practices and perspectives.

UNDERSTANDING ENERGY PROTECTION: Energy protection involves creating a shield or barrier around one's energy field to prevent unwanted influences, negative vibrations, and psychic intrusions from external sources (Gerber, 2001).

IT IS BASED on the principle that the human energy field is permeable and can be affected by the thoughts, emotions, and energies of others. Energy protection techniques help maintain boundaries and preserve the integrity of one's own energy system (McCarthy, 2010).

Practices for Energy Protection

- **Visualisation:** Visualisation techniques involve imagining a protective shield of light surrounding the body, creating a barrier that repels negativity and maintains energetic integrity (Eden, 2008).

- **Grounding:** Grounding practices involve connecting with the Earth's energy, anchoring oneself in the present moment, and releasing excess energy or tension into the ground (Hartley, 1999).

- **Auric Cleansing:** Auric cleansing techniques involve clearing and purifying the energy field, removing stagnant or negative energies that may accumulate over time (Brinkley, 2003).

- **Setting Boundaries:** Setting energetic boundaries involves consciously establishing limits and asserting one's needs and preferences in relationships and interactions (Mate, 2003).

- **Protective Crystals:** Crystals such as black tourmaline, obsidian, and amethyst are believed to have protective properties that can shield the energy field and deflect negative influences (Gienger, 2013).

- **Sound Healing:** Sound healing techniques, including chanting, drumming, and toning, can clear and harmonise the energy field, restoring balance and promoting inner peace (Halpern, 2010).

- **Intention and Affirmation:** Intention is a powerful tool for energy protection, as it focuses the mind and directs energy toward a specific outcome. Setting clear intentions for protection and invoking divine guidance can enhance the effectiveness of energy protection practices (Dossey, 2009).

- Affirmations are positive statements that affirm one's power, sovereignty, and connection to divine protection. By repeating affirmations regularly, individuals can strengthen their energetic boundaries and cultivate a sense of inner strength and resilience (Hay, 2008).

- **Integration and Self-Care:** Energy protection is an ongoing practice that requires self-awareness, mindfulness, and self-care. Integrating energy protection techniques into daily routines and rituals can support holistic well-being and promote a sense of empowerment and sovereignty (McTaggart, 2007).

Conclusion

Harnessing energy for protection and preservation is an essential aspect of holistic living and spiritual growth. By cultivating awareness of one's own energy field and implementing protective practices, individuals can create a sanctuary of peace, balance, and harmony amidst the challenges of daily life.

The Calming Influence of Nature: Energy, Vibration, and Elemental Harmony

Nature has long been recognised as a source of solace, tranquility, and rejuvenation for the human spirit. In this chapter, we explore the multifaceted reasons why nature exerts a calming force on the mind, drawing from the principles of energy, vibration, stillness, and the quality of air.

ENERGY AND VIBRATION: Nature is imbued with a subtle energy that resonates with the human psyche and spirit. The vibrant life force present in natural landscapes, from towering trees to babbling brooks, emanates a harmonious vibration that uplifts the soul and restores balance (Kellert & Wilson, 1993).

THE EARTH itself is a living organism with its own energetic frequency, known as the Schumann Resonance. This resonant frequency, approximately 7.83 Hz, mirrors the human brain's alpha wave state and is believed to promote feelings of relaxation, well-being, and connection to the Earth (Bergquist, 2004).

STILLNESS AND SERENITY: Nature provides a sanctuary of stillness and serenity amidst the hustle and bustle of modern life. The tranquil beauty of natural landscapes, from majestic mountains to serene seascapes, invites individuals to slow down, breathe deeply, and attune to the rhythm of the natural world (Kaplan, 1995).

THE ABSENCE of man-made noise and distractions in natural environments allows the mind to quieten, facilitating a sense of inner peace, clarity, and presence. This state of stillness opens the door to contemplation, introspection, and connection with the deeper dimensions of the self (Mayer, 2009).

. . .

QUALITY OF AIR AND VITALITY: The air in natural environments is imbued with purity, freshness, and vitality, enriched by the oxygen released through photosynthesis and the negative ions generated by flowing water and abundant foliage (Bowler et al., 2010).

BREATHING IN THE CRISP, clean air of natural settings promotes oxygenation of the brain and body, invigorating the senses, enhancing mental clarity, and boosting overall well-being. The inhalation of phytoncides, natural compounds emitted by trees and plants, has been shown to reduce stress levels and strengthen the immune system (Li et al., 2009).

BIOPHILIA AND EVOLUTIONARY CONNECTION: Humans have an innate affinity for nature, known as biophilia, which reflects our evolutionary connection to the natural world (Wilson, 1984). Throughout history, our ancestors lived in close harmony with nature, deriving sustenance, shelter, and spiritual nourishment from the land.

BIOPHILIC EXPERIENCES, such as walking in the woods, gazing at starlit skies, or listening to birdsong, evoke primal memories of our evolutionary past, activating neural pathways associated with relaxation, awe, and wonder (Ulrich, 1984).

CONCLUSION

The calming force of nature stems from its inherent energy, vibration, stillness, and vitality, which resonate with the deepest recesses of the human soul. By immersing ourselves in the natural world, we can tap into its transformative power, finding solace, inspiration, and renewal amidst the beauty and majesty of creation.

8

TRANSFORMATION AND MANIFESTATION

The Power of Positive Thinking: Transforming Consciousness and Raising your Frequency

In the vast landscape of human consciousness, the power of positive thinking stands as a beacon of transformative potential, offering individuals a pathway to cultivate optimism, resilience, and abundance. Rooted in the principles of the Law of Attraction theory, positive thinking transcends mere optimism to shape the very fabric of reality. In this article, we explore the profound influence of positive thinking on consciousness, delve into the core tenets of the Law of Attraction, and offer practical strategies to adjust a negative mindset.

Understanding Positive Thinking and Consciousness

Positive thinking is more than just a mindset—it is a way of being that fosters a deep alignment with the inherent goodness and potentiality of life. At its core, positive thinking involves cultivating thoughts, beliefs, and attitudes that affirm abundance, possibility, and empowerment (Seligman, 2006). By directing attention and intention towards positive outcomes, individuals can shape their reality and harness the creative power of consciousness.

The Law of Attraction: Manifesting Thoughts into Reality

The Law of Attraction, a cornerstone of metaphysical philosophy, posits that like attracts like—that is, thoughts and beliefs have the power to manifest corresponding experiences and circumstances (Hicks & Hicks, 2004). According to this principle, the universe is a vast field of energy and consciousness that responds to the vibrational frequencies emitted by individuals. By aligning thoughts, emotions, and actions with desired outcomes, individuals can magnetise opportunities, relationships, and abundance into their lives.

PRACTICAL STRATEGIES TO Adjust a Negative Mindset

- **Cultivate Self-Awareness**: Begin by cultivating awareness of negative thought patterns and limiting beliefs. Notice when negative thoughts arise and observe their impact on emotions, behaviour, and well-being. Self-awareness is the first step towards transformation.

- **Practice Gratitude:** Cultivate an attitude of gratitude by focusing on blessings, abundance, and moments of joy in everyday life. Keep a gratitude journal, where you regularly write down things you are thankful for. Gratitude shifts the focus from scarcity to abundance, fostering a positive outlook on life (Emmons & McCullough, 2003).

- **Affirmations and Visualisation:** Harness the power of affirmations and visualisation to reprogram the subconscious mind and align with desired outcomes. Create affirmations that affirm positive beliefs and intentions, and visualise yourself living the life you desire with vivid detail and emotion.

- **Surround Yourself with Positivity:** Surround yourself with positive influences, supportive relationships, and uplifting environments. Limit exposure to negative news, media, and toxic relationships that drain energy and perpetuate negativity.

- **Practice Mindfulness and Meditation:** Cultivate mindfulness and meditation practices to cultivate inner peace, presence, and clarity of mind. Mindfulness allows you to observe thoughts without attachment, fostering a sense of equanimity and resilience in the face of challenges (Kabat-Zinn, 2003).

CONCLUSION

The power of positive thinking is a potent force that shapes consciousness, transforms reality, and unlocks the inherent potential of the human spirit. By embracing optimism, aligning with the Law of Attraction, and practicing practical strategies to adjust a negative mindset, individuals can cultivate a life of abundance, joy, and fulfilment.

Elevating Your Vibrational Frequency: Living Authentically for Happiness, Abundance, and Prosperity

Living authentically and aligning with a higher vibrational frequency is key to unlocking a life filled with happiness, abundance, and prosperity. In this chapter, we explore practical strategies and insights to elevate your vibrational frequency and cultivate a life that resonates with authenticity and fulfilment.

Understanding Vibrational Frequency

Vibrational frequency refers to the energetic signature or resonance emitted by individuals, influenced by thoughts, emotions, beliefs, and actions (Dispenza, 2017). Higher vibrational frequencies are associated with states of joy, love, gratitude, and empowerment, while lower frequencies are linked to fear, doubt, and lack.

EMBRACE Authenticity and Self-Expression

Know Thyself: Self-awareness is the foundation of authenticity. Take time for introspection, reflection, and exploration to uncover your true values, passions, and aspirations (Brown, 2012). Embrace your unique strengths, quirks, and imperfections as part of your authentic self.

Live Your Truth: Authentic living requires courage and vulnerability. Be honest with yourself and others about your feelings, desires, and boundaries. Express your true thoughts and emotions authentically, without fear of judgment or rejection (Brown, 2010).

Cultivate Positive Thoughts and Beliefs

Practice Gratitude: Cultivate an attitude of gratitude by focusing on blessings, abundance, and moments of joy in everyday life. Gratitude elevates your vibrational frequency, fosters a positive outlook, and attracts more blessings into your life (Emmons, 2007).

Affirmations and Visualisation: Use positive affirmations and visualisation techniques to reprogram your subconscious mind and align with your desired reality (Hay, 1984). Affirmations reinforce empowering beliefs and intentions, while visualisation activates the creative power of the imagination.

Nurture Positive Relationships and Connections

Surround Yourself with Positivity: Surround yourself with supportive relationships, uplifting environments, and inspirational role models. Cultivate connections with individuals who uplift and inspire you to be your best self (Hicks & Hicks, 2004).

Serve Others: Practice acts of kindness, compassion, and service to others. Giving and receiving love, support, and generosity elevates your vibrational frequency and creates a ripple effect of positivity and abundance in the world (Post, 2005).

Embrace Growth and Expansion

Embrace Challenges as Opportunities: View challenges and setbacks as opportunities for growth, learning, and transformation. Embrace discomfort and uncertainty as catalysts for personal and spiritual evolution (Dweck, 2006).

Continuous Learning and Development: Cultivate a growth mindset and a thirst for knowledge, learning, and self-improvement. Engage in lifelong learning, pursue passions and interests, and expand your horizons to unlock new possibilities and potentials (Dweck, 2016).

Conclusion
Elevating your vibrational frequency and living authentically are transformative practices that empower you to create a life of happiness, abundance, and prosperity. By embracing authenticity, cultivating positive thoughts and beliefs, nurturing meaningful relationships, and embracing growth and expansion, you align with the highest version of yourself and manifest your deepest desires and aspirations.

The Potential of an Enlightened Society: Transforming the World as We Know It

Imagine a world where compassion, wisdom, and interconnectedness are the guiding principles of society—a world where every individual is empowered to live authentically, express their highest potential, and contribute to the greater good. In this chapter, we explore the profound impact of an enlightened society and the transformative changes it can bring about in the world.

. . .

Vision of an Enlightened Society

Cultivating Inner Wisdom: In an enlightened society, individuals are encouraged to cultivate inner wisdom through mindfulness practices, self-reflection, and spiritual exploration (Kabat-Zinn, 1994). By accessing the depths of their own consciousness, individuals gain insight, clarity, and a deeper understanding of themselves and the world around them.

Embracing Diversity and Inclusivity: An enlightened society celebrates diversity and honours the inherent worth and dignity of every individual (Putnam, 2007). It fosters a culture of inclusivity, respect, and acceptance, where people of all backgrounds, beliefs, and identities are welcomed and valued.

Promoting Social Justice and Equality: Social justice and equality are foundational values in an enlightened society (Rawls, 1971). It seeks to dismantle systems of oppression, discrimination, and inequality, and strives to create a more just, equitable, and compassionate world for all.

Transformative Changes in an Enlightened Society

Shift in Consciousness: An enlightened society catalyses a shift in collective consciousness, from fear, separation, and scarcity to love, unity, and abundance (Wilber, 2007). It acknowledges the interconnectedness of all life and recognises that every thought, word, and action has ripple effects that reverberate throughout the world.

Holistic Education and Lifelong Learning: Education in an enlightened society goes beyond academic knowledge and emphasises holistic development of the mind, body, and spirit

(Noddings, 2005). It fosters critical thinking, creativity, empathy, and emotional intelligence, empowering individuals to navigate life's challenges with resilience and compassion.

Sustainable Living and Environmental Stewardship: An enlightened society values the interconnectedness of humanity and the natural world (Berry, 2009). It adopts sustainable practices, conserves resources, and promotes environmental stewardship to ensure a thriving planet for future generations.

Collaborative Governance and Decision-Making: Governance in an enlightened society is participatory, transparent, and inclusive (Eckersley, 2004). It engages citizens in decision-making processes, fosters dialogue and consensus-building, and prioritises the common good over narrow self-interests.

Realising the Vision

Creating an enlightened society is a collective endeavour that requires the commitment and collaboration of individuals, communities, and institutions (Senge et al., 2008). By embodying the principles of compassion, wisdom, and interconnectedness in our daily lives, we contribute to the gradual unfolding of a more enlightened world.

Conclusion

An enlightened society holds the potential to transform the world as we know it, ushering in an era of peace, harmony, and prosperity for all beings. By embracing the values of compassion, wisdom, and interconnectedness, and working together to address the pressing challenges of our time, we can co-create a brighter, more compassionate future for generations to come.

REFERENCES

- Abram, D. (1997). The Spell of the Sensuous: Perception and Language in a More-Than-Human World. Vintage.
- Alam, M. (2016). The impact of vibration on the human body. In Mechanical Vibration and Shock Analysis, Volume 5: Specification Development (pp. 1-29). John Wiley & Sons.
- Assagioli, R. (1973). The act of will. Penguin.
- Astin, J. A., et al. (2003). The Efficacy of Mindfulness Meditation Plus Qigong Movement Therapy in the Treatment of Fibromyalgia: A Randomized Controlled Trial. The Journal of Rheumatology.
- Baars, B. J. (1988). A cognitive theory of consciousness. Cambridge University Press.
- Baker, K. G., Robertson, V. J., & Duck, F. A. (2001). A review of therapeutic ultrasound: biophysical effects. Physical Therapy, 81(7), 1351-1358.
- Baldwin, A. L., Schwartz, G. E., & Schwartz, J. (2013). Energy psychology: self-healing practices for bodymind health. TarcherPerigee.
- Barker, S. B., & Dawson, K. S. (1998). The Effects of Animal-Assisted Therapy on Anxiety Ratings of Hospitalised Psychiatric Patients. Psychiatric Services.
- Battista, A., & Tattelman, E. (2017). The Scent of the Soul: Exploring the Spiritual and Aromatic Dimensions of Essential Oils. Simon and Schuster.
- Beck, A. M. (2012). The Biology of the Human-Animal Bond. Animal Frontiers.
- Becker, R. O., & Hagens, P. (1981). The Body Electric: Electromagnetism and the Foundation of Life. William Morrow and Company.
- Begay, David, and Rina Swentzell. (2002). Navajo and Pueblo Sacred Places. Indiana University Press.
- Bergquist, M. (2004). The Earth's Resonant Frequency. Journal of Scientific Exploration.
- Berndt, R. M., & Berndt, C. H. (1977). The World of the First Australians: An Introduction to the Traditional Life of the Australian Aborigines. University of Chicago Press.
- Berry, T. (2009). The Great Work: Our Way into the Future. Convergent Books.
- Blank, M., & Goodman, R. (2009). Electromagnetic Fields and Health: DNA-Based Dosimetry. Springer.
- Boardman, J. (2000). The history of Greek vases. Thames & Hudson.
- Boly, M., Coleman, M. R., Davis, M. H., Hampshire, A., Bor, D., Moonen, G., ... & Pickard, J. D. (2007). When thoughts become action: An fMRI paradigm to

study volitional brain activity in non-communicative brain injured patients. NeuroImage, 36(3), 979-992.

- Bowler, D. E., et al. (2010). A Systematic Review of Evidence for the Added Benefits to Health of Exposure to Natural Environments. BMC Public Health.

- Bratman, G. N., et al. (2012). Nature Experience Reduces Rumination and Subgenual Prefrontal Cortex Activation. Proceedings of the National Academy of Sciences.

- Braud, W., & Anderson, R. (1998). Transpersonal research methods for the social sciences: Honoring human experience. Sage Publications.

- Braun, V., Clarke, V., & Gray, D. (2008). Collecting Qualitative Data: A Practical Guide to Textual, Media and Virtual Techniques. Cambridge University Press.

- Brennan, B. (1987). Hands of Light: A Guide to Healing Through the Human Energy Field. Bantam.

- Brennan, B. (1993). Light Emerging: The Journey of Personal Healing. Bantam.

- Brewer, J. A., Worhunsky, P. D., Gray, J. R., Tang, Y. Y., Weber, J., & Kober, H. (2011). Meditation experience is associated with differences in default mode network activity and connectivity. Proceedings of the National Academy of Sciences, 108(50), 20254-20259.

- Brinkley, V. (2003). Cleansing the Doors of Perception: The Religious Significance of Entheogenic Plants and Chemicals. Sentient Publications.

- Brock, A. (2018). Digital Divide: Civic Engagement, Information Poverty, and the Internet Worldwide. Oxford University Press.

- Brown, B. (2010). The Gifts of Imperfection: Let Go of Who You Think You're Supposed to Be and Embrace Who You Are. Hazelden Publishing.

- Brown, B. (2012). Daring Greatly: How the Courage to Be Vulnerable Transforms the Way We Live, Love, Parent, and Lead. Avery.

- Bruce, R. (1999). Astral Dynamics: The Complete Book of Out-of-Body Experiences. Hampton Roads Publishing.

- Buchbauer, G. (1993). Aromatherapy: Evidence for Sedative Effects of the Essential Oil of Lavender after Inhalation. Zeitschrift Für Naturforschung C.

- Buckle, J. (2003). Clinical Aromatherapy: Essential Oils in Practice. Churchill Livingstone.

- Budilovsky, J., & Adamson, E. (2000). The Complete Idiot's Guide to Yoga. Penguin.

- Burkert, W. (1985). Greek Religion. Harvard University Press.

- Buzsáki, G., & Draguhn, A. (2004). Neuronal Oscillations in Cortical Networks. Science, 304(5679), 1926–1929. doi:10.1126/science.1099745)

- Buzsáki, G., & Draguhn, A. (2004). Neuronal Oscillations in Cortical Networks. Science.

- Cajochen, C., et al. (2013). Evidence that the Lunar Cycle Influences Human Sleep. Current Biology.
- Camus, A. (1942). The Myth of Sisyphus. Vintage.
- Capra, F. (1975). The Tao of Physics: An Exploration of the Parallels between Modern Physics and Eastern Mysticism. Shambhala.
- Carhart-Harris, R. L., Erritzoe, D., Williams, T., Stone, J. M., Reed, L. J., Colasanti, A., ... & Hobden, P. (2012). Neural correlates of the psychedelic state as determined by fMRI studies with psilocybin. Proceedings of the National Academy of Sciences, 109(6), 2138-2143.
- Castells, M. (1996). The Rise of the Network Society. Wiley-Blackwell.
- Chalmers, D. J. (1995). Facing up to the problem of consciousness. Journal of Consciousness Studies, 2(3), 200-219.
- Chalmers, D. J. (1995). Facing Up to the Problem of Consciousness. Journal of Consciousness Studies.
- Chang, C. Y., et al. (2014). Vibroacoustic Sound Therapy Improves Pain and Muscle Stiffness in Patients Undergoing Total Knee Arthroplasty: A Randomised Controlled Trial. Journal of Clinical Nursing.
- Chang, H., et al. (2012). The Effects of Music on the Autonomic Nervous System and Electroencephalogram of Healthy Individuals: A Comparison of Mozart and Pop Music. Journal of the Formosan Medical Association.
- Chang, K. M., Chao, H. T., Huang, S. C., & Lin, C. Y. (2019). Effect of Gong Sound Meditation on Cognitive Function, Quality of Life, and Stress in Older Adults. Journal of Holistic Nursing.
- Chiesa, A., & Malinowski, P. (2011). Mindfulness-based approaches: are they all the same? Journal of Clinical Psychology, 67(4), 404-424.
- Chopra, D. (1994). The Seven Spiritual Laws of Success. New World Library.
- Chulliat, A., et al. (2019). World Magnetic Model for 2015–2020: spherical harmonic coefficients, time derivatives, and long-term secular variation predictions. Earth, Planets and Space.
- Collins, T. (2011). The Power of the Gong: Sound Healing, Transformation, and Enlightenment. Healing Arts Press.
- Collins, T. (2011). The Way of the Gong: An Archetypal Journey.
- 1 Corinthians 11:23-26: The Holy Bible: New International Version. Biblica, 2011.
- Crenshaw, K. (2017). On Intersectionality: Essential Writings. The New Press.
- Cross, I. (2014). Music and Social Interaction. In The Social Psychology of Music.
- Cunningham, S. (2002). Cunningham's Encyclopedia of Crystal, Gem & Metal Magic. Llewellyn Publications.
- Cutler, W. B., et al. (1987). The Psychoneuroendocrinology of the Menstrual Cycle. In Psychoneuroendocrinology in Reproduction.

- Dale, C. (2001). The Subtle Body: An Encyclopedia of Your Energetic Anatomy. Sounds True.
- Daubenmire, R. (1956). Plants and Environment: A Textbook of Plant Autecology. John Wiley & Sons.
- Davidson, R. J., et al. (2003). Alterations in Brain and Immune Function Produced by Mindfulness Meditation. Psychosomatic Medicine.
- Deacon, T. (1997). The Symbolic Species: The Co-Evolution of Language and the Brain. W. W. Norton & Company.
- Dennett, D. C. (1991). Consciousness Explained. Little, Brown and Company.
- Descartes, R. (1641). Meditations on First Philosophy.
- Diamond, J. (1997). Guns, Germs, and Steel: The Fates of Human Societies. W. W. Norton & Company.
- DiAngelo, R. (2018). White Fragility: Why It's So Hard for White People to Talk About Racism. Beacon Press.
- Dicke, M., & Baldwin, I. T. (2010). The Plant's Enemy: Chemical Defense against Herbivores. Science.
- Dispenza, J. (2012). Breaking the Habit of Being Yourself: How to Lose Your Mind and Create a New One. Hay House.
- Dispenza, J. (2017). Becoming Supernatural: How Common People Are Doing the Uncommon. Hay House.
- Dodds, E. R. (1951). The Greeks and the irrational. University of California Press.
- Doidge, N. (2007). The Brain That Changes Itself: Stories of Personal Triumph from the Frontiers of Brain Science. Penguin Books.
- Dossey, L. (1999). Reinventing Medicine: Beyond Mind-Body to a New Era of Healing. HarperOne.
- Dossey, L. (2009). The Power of Premonitions: How Knowing the Future Can Shape Our Lives. Penguin.
- Dossey, L. (2013). One Mind: How Our Individual Mind Is Part of a Greater Consciousness and Why It Matters. Hay House, Inc.
- Dunbar, R. I. M. (1998). Grooming, Gossip, and the Evolution of Language. Harvard University Press.
- Dweck, C. (2006). Mindset: The New Psychology of Success. Random House.
- Dweck, C. (2016). Mindset: Changing the Way You Think to Fulfil Your Potential. Robinson.
- Eason, C. (2015). The Complete Crystal Handbook: Your Guide to More than 500 Crystals. Sterling Ethos.
- Eberhardt, J. L. (2019). Biased: Uncovering the Hidden Prejudice That Shapes What We See, Think, and Do. Viking.
- Eckersley, R. (2004). The Green State: Rethinking Democracy and Sovereignty. MIT Press.

- Eden, D. (2008). Energy Medicine: Balancing Your Body's Energies for Optimal Health, Joy, and Vitality. TarcherPerigee.
- Eisenstein, C. (2011). Sacred Economics: Money, Gift, and Society in the Age of Transition. North Atlantic Books.
- Eisler, R. (1987). The Chalice and the Blade: Our History, Our Future. HarperOne.
- Ekman, P. (1992). An Argument for Basic Emotions. Cognition & Emotion.
- Emmons, R. A. (2007). Thanks!: How the New Science of Gratitude Can Make You Happier. Houghton Mifflin Harcourt.
- Emmons, R. A., & McCullough, M. E. (2003). Counting Blessings Versus Burdens: An Experimental Investigation of Gratitude and Subjective Well-Being in Daily Life. Journal of Personality and Social Psychology.
- Feynman, Richard P., et al. The Feynman Lectures on Physics. Basic Books, 2011.
- Fine, A. H. (2010). Handbook on Animal-Assisted Therapy: Theoretical Foundations and Guidelines for Practice. Academic Press.
- Fine, A. H. (2015). Handbook on Animal-Assisted Therapy: Foundations and Guidelines for Animal-Assisted Interventions. Academic Press.
- Finlay, C. C., et al. (2016). International Geomagnetic Reference Field: the eleventh generation. Geophysical Journal International.
- Flood, G. (1996). An Introduction to Hinduism. Cambridge University Press.
- Fontenrose, J. E. (1978). Python: A study of Delphic myth and its origins. University of California Press.
- Foster, R. G. (2013). Sleep and Circadian Rhythms: Regulating the Rhythm of Life. Springer Science & Business Media.
- Fox, K. C., et al. (2014). Is Meditation Associated with Altered Brain Structure? A Systematic Review and Meta-Analysis of Morphometric Neuroimaging in Meditation Practitioners. Neuroscience & Biobehavioral Reviews.
- Frawley, D., & Summerfield Kozak, S. (2002). Yoga for Your Type: An Ayurvedic Approach to Your Asana Practice. Lotus Press.
- Frawley, David, and Vasant Lad. (1994). The Yoga of Herbs: An Ayurvedic Guide to Herbal Medicine. Lotus Press.
- Frawley, David. (2000). Ayurveda and the Mind: The Healing of Consciousness. Lotus Press.
- Frede, D. (1987). The original notion of cause. In M. L. Gill & P. Pellegrin (Eds.), A companion to ancient philosophy (pp. 285-308). Wiley-Blackwell.
- Freud, S. (1900). The Interpretation of Dreams. Basic Books.
- Freud, S. (1915). The unconscious. Standard Edition, 14, 166-204.
- Freud, S. (1915). The Unconscious. The Hogarth Press.
- Fröhlich, H. (1980). Biological Coherence and Response to External Stimuli. Springer.

- Fromm, J., & Lautner, S. (2007). Electrical Signals and Their Physiological Significance in Plants. Plant, Cell & Environment.
- Gagliano, M. (2014). In a Green Frame of Mind: Perspectives on the Behavioral Ecology and Cognitive Nature of Plants. AoB Plants.
- Gagliano, M., et al. (2017). Green symphonies: a call for studies on acoustic communication in plants. Behavioral Ecology.
- Gardner, K. (1990). The Sacred Geography of Sound: The Transformation of Consciousness in Chanting. Ethos.
- Garfield, P. (1998). Pathway to Ecstasy: The Way of the Dream Mandala. New World Library.
- Gassmann, D., et al. (2013). Music Medicine: The Science and Spirit of Healing Yourself with Sound. Sounds True.
- Gerber, R. (2001). Vibrational Medicine: The #1 Handbook of Subtle-Energy Therapies. Bear & Company.
- Gienger, M. (2013). Healing Crystals: The A-Z Guide to 430 Gemstones. Earthdancer.
- Gienger, M. (2013). Healing Crystals: The A-Z Guide to 555 Gemstones. Hauppauge, NY: Barron's Educational Series.
- Gill, Sam D. (1997). Sacred Words: A Study of Navajo Religion and Prayer. University of Arizona Press.
- Gleiser, M. (2019). The Simple Beauty of the Unexpected: A Natural Philosopher's Quest for Trout and the Meaning of Everything. Farrar, Straus and Giroux.
- Goldman, J. (2003). Healing Sounds: The Power of Harmonics. Healing Arts Press.
- Goldman, J. (2011). The Divine Name: The Sound That Can Change the World. Hay House.
- Goldstein, J., & Kornfield, J. (2002). Seeking the Heart of Wisdom: The Path of Insight Meditation. Shambhala Publications.
- Goleman, D. (1995). Emotional Intelligence: Why It Can Matter More Than IQ. Bantam Books.
- Goleman, D., & Schwartz, G. (1976). Meditation as an Intervention in Stress Reactivity. Journal of Consulting and Clinical Psychology.
- Goswami, A. (1995). The Self-Aware Universe: How Consciousness Creates the Material World. Penguin.
- Greene, B. (1999). The elegant universe: Superstrings, hidden dimensions, and the quest for the ultimate theory. W. W. Norton & Company.
- Greene, B. (2011). The Hidden Reality: Parallel Universes and the Deep Laws of the Cosmos. Vintage Books.
- Greene, L. (1985). The Astrology of Fate. Bantam Books.

- Grenz, Stanley J. *Theology for the Community of God*. Wm. B. Eerdmans Publishing Co., 2000.
- Grof, S. (2000). Psychology of the Future: Lessons from Modern Consciousness Research. State University of New York Press.
- Grof, S. (2006). The cosmic game: Explorations of the frontiers of human consciousness. SUNY Press.
- Gubbins, D. (2011). Encyclopedia of Geomagnetism and Paleomagnetism. Springer.
- Gyatso, J. (1992). In the Mirror of Memory: Reflections on Mindfulness and Remembrance in Indian and Tibetan Buddhism. State University of New York Press.
- Haddock, S. H., et al. (2010). Bioluminescence in the Sea. Annual Review of Marine Science.
- Hagelin, J. S. (1994). Is Consciousness the Unified Field? A Field Theorist's Perspective. Modern Physics Letters A.
- Hall, J. (2009). The Crystal Bible: A Definitive Guide to Crystals. London: Godsfield Press.
- Hall, J. (2011). The Crystal Bible: A Definitive Guide to Crystals. Godsfield Press.
- Halliday, David, et al. Fundamentals of Physics. Wiley, 2013.
- Halpern, P. (2012). The Cosmic Symphony: The Vibrating Universe. Oxford University Press.
- Halpern, S. (2010). Sound Healing: Vibrational Healing with Ohm Tuning Forks. Healing Arts Press.
- Halpern, S. H. (2014). Sound Health: The Music and Sounds That Make Us Whole. HarperOne.
- Hameroff, S., & Penrose, R. (1996). Conscious Events as Orchestrated Space-Time Selections. Journal of Consciousness Studies.
- Hammer, A. (2012). Clinical Applications of Music Therapy in Psychiatry. Jessica Kingsley Publishers.
- Hanh, T. N. (2012). Peace Is Every Step: The Path of Mindfulness in Everyday Life. Bantam.
- Hankinson, R. J. (1998). Cause and explanation in ancient Greek thought. Oxford University Press.
- Harari, Y. N. (2014). Sapiens: A Brief History of Humankind. Harper.
- Harari, Y. N. (2016). Homo Deus: A Brief History of Tomorrow. Harper.
- Harner, M. (1982). The Way of the Shaman: A Guide to Power and Healing. HarperOne.
- Hartley, L. (1999). Grounded in the Gospel: Building Believers the Old-Fashioned Way. Moody Publishers.
- Hartmann, G. (1989). Earth Grids: The Secret Patterns of Gaia's Sacred Sites. Harper Collins.

- Hasegawa, T., Amano, K., Nakamura, T., Ishihara, M., & Sawada, Y. (2019). Effects of Ultrasound Therapy on Bone Healing. Ultrasound in Medicine & Biology, 45(12), 3062-3070.
- Hassed, C., et al. (2015). Mindfulness: Allowing an Effective Response to Complexity in Leadership. Integral Leadership Review.
- Hawken, P. (2007). Blessed Unrest: How the Largest Movement in the World Came into Being and Why No One Saw It Coming. Penguin.
- Hawking, S. (1988). A Brief History of Time: From the Big Bang to Black Holes. Bantam Books.
- Hay, L. (1984). You Can Heal Your Life. Hay House.
- Hay, L. (2008). Experience Your Good Now!: Learning to Use Affirmations. Hay House Inc.
- Herculano-Houzel, S. (2011). Scaling of Brain Metabolism with a Fixed Energy Budget per Neuron: Implications for Neuronal Activity, Plasticity and Evolution. PLoS ONE, 6(3), e17514. doi:10.1371/journal.pone.0017514;
- Hess, A. (2017). The Rise of Victimhood Culture: Microaggressions, Safe Spaces, and the New Culture Wars. Palgrave Macmillan.
- Hess, D. (2016). The Gong: An Ancient Instrument of Healing. White Cloud Press.
- Hess, J. (2016). Sacred Sound: Discovering the Myth and Meaning of Music in World Religions.
- Hicks, E., & Hicks, J. (2004). The Law of Attraction: The Basics of the Teachings of Abraham. Hay House.
- Hobson, J. A. (2002). Dreaming: An Introduction to the Science of Sleep. Oxford University Press.
- Hoffmann, D. (2003). Medical Herbalism: The Science Principles and Practices of Herbal Medicine. Healing Arts Press.
- Hölzel, B. K., et al. (2011). Mindfulness Practice Leads to Increases in Regional Brain Gray Matter Density. Psychiatry Research.
- Horton, J., et al. (2020). Predicting extreme geomagnetic activity using coronal mass ejection properties and solar wind speeds. Space Weather.
- Hunt, V. V. (1995). Infinite Mind: Science of the Human Vibrations of Consciousness. Malibu Publishing Company.
- Inwood, B. (2007). The Stoics reader: Selected writings and testimonia. Hackett Publishing.
- Iyengar, B. K. S. (2001). Light on Yoga. HarperCollins.
- Jahnke, R. (2002). The healing promise of Qi: Creating extraordinary wellness through Qigong and Tai Chi. McGraw-Hill Education.
- James 5:14-15: The Holy Bible: New International Version. Biblica, 2011.
- James, W. (1902). The varieties of religious experience. Longmans, Green & Co.
- Jansen, J. (2017). Tibetan Sound Healing: Seven Guided Practices to Clear

Obstacles, Cultivate Positive Qualities, and Uncover Your Inherent Wisdom. Sounds True.

- John 14:16-17: The Holy Bible: New International Version. Biblica, 2011.
- Judith, A. (2004). Wheels of Life: A User's Guide to the Chakra System. Llewellyn Publications.
- Jung, C. G. (1932). Commentary on The Secret of the Golden Flower. Pantheon Books.
- Jung, C. G. (1933). Modern Man in Search of a Soul. Harcourt Brace.
- Jung, C. G. (1953). Psychology and Alchemy.
- Jung, C. G. (1959). The archetypes and the collective unconscious (R. F. C. Hull, Trans.). Princeton University Press.
- Jung, C. G. (1959). The Archetypes and the Collective Unconscious. Princeton University Press.
- Jung, C. G. (1968). Man and His Symbols. Doubleday.
- Jung, C. G. (1968). The Archetypes and the Collective Unconscious (R. F. C. Hull, Trans.). Princeton University Press.
- Jung, C. G. (1971). Psychological Types. Princeton University Press.
- Kabat-Zinn, J. (1990). Full Catastrophe Living: Using the Wisdom of Your Body and Mind to Face Stress, Pain, and Illness. Bantam Dell.
- Kabat-Zinn, J. (1994). Wherever You Go, There You Are: Mindfulness Meditation in Everyday Life. Hyperion.
- Kabat-Zinn, J. (2003). Mindfulness-Based Interventions in Context: Past, Present, and Future. Clinical Psychology: Science and Practice.
- Kakar, S. (1989). The Inner World: A Psychoanalytic Study of Childhood and Society in India. Oxford University Press.
- Kaku, M. (2005). Parallel worlds: A journey through creation, higher dimensions, and the future of the cosmos. Anchor Books.
- Kaminski, P., & Katz, R. (2000). Flower Essence Repertory: A Comprehensive Guide to North American and English Flower Essences for Emotional and Spiritual Well-Being. Flower Essence Society.
- Kaplan, R. (1995). The Restorative Benefits of Nature: Toward an Integrative Framework. Journal of Environmental Psychology.
- Kaptchuk, T. J. (2002). Acupuncture: Theory, efficacy, and practice. Annals of Internal Medicine, 136(5), 374-383.
- Karban, R. (2008). Plant Behaviour and Communication. Ecology Letters.
- Kellert, S. R., & Wilson, E. O. (1993). The Biophilia Hypothesis. Island Press.
- Kendi, I. X. (2019). How to Be an Antiracist. One World.
- Khalsa, Shakti Parwha Kaur. Kundalini Yoga: The Flow of Eternal Power. Kundalini Research Institute, 1996.
- Khan-Cullors, P., & Bandele, A. (2017). When They Call You a Terrorist: A Black Lives Matter Memoir. St. Martin's Press.

- Klein, N. (2014). This Changes Everything: Capitalism vs. The Climate. Simon & Schuster.
- Klein, N. (2019). On Fire: The (Burning) Case for a Green New Deal. Simon & Schuster.
- Koch, C. (2004). The Quest for Consciousness: A Neurobiological Approach. Roberts & Company Publishers.
- Köhnke, C. (2005). The Influence of Lunar Phases on the Birth-Rate. Psychological Reports.
- Krause, B. (2012). The Great Animal Orchestra: Finding the Origins of Music in the World's Wild Places. Little, Brown and Company.
- Krause, B., & Rabinowitz, A. (2019). The Great Animal Orchestra: Discovering the Origins of Music in the World's Wild Places. Profile Books.
- Krishna, G. (1993). Kundalini: The Evolutionary Energy in Man. Shambhala Publications.
- Kumar, K. (2018). The Rise of the Alt-Right. Lexington Books.
- Kumar, V., & Fouad, H. (2016). Fundamentals of Light and Optics. CRC Press.
- Kuriyama, S. (1999). The expressiveness of the body and the divergence of Greek and Chinese medicine. New Literary History, 30(4), 739-763.
- LaBerge, S. (1985). Lucid Dreaming. Ballantine Books.
- Lad, V. (1999). Textbook of Ayurveda. Ayurvedic Press.
- Lad, Vasant. (2001). The Complete Book of Ayurvedic Home Remedies. Three Rivers Press.
- Lad, Vasant. (2002). Textbook of Ayurveda, Volume 1: Fundamental Principles. Ayurvedic Press.
- Lanza, R., & Berman, B. (2009). Biocentrism: How Life and Consciousness Are the Keys to Understanding the True Nature of the Universe. BenBella Books.
- Laozi. (6th century BCE). Tao Te Ching.
- Laundal, K. M., & Richmond, A. D. (2017). Magnetic Coordinate Systems. Space Science Reviews.
- Laureys, S., Owen, A. M., & Schiff, N. D. (2004). Brain function in coma, vegetative state, and related disorders. The Lancet Neurology, 3(9), 537-546.
- Lawless, J. (2001). The Encyclopedia of Essential Oils: The Complete Guide to the Use of Aromatic Oils in Aromatherapy, Herbalism, Health, and Wellbeing. Conari Press.
- Lay, T., et al. (2010). Modern Global Seismology. Academic Press.
- Leadbeater, C. W., & Besant, A. (1895). Man: Visible and invisible. Theosophical Publishing Society.
- Lebedev, A. V., Kaelen, M., Lövdén, M., Nilsson, J., Feilding, A., Nutt, D. J., & Carhart-Harris, R. L. (2015). LSD-induced entropic brain activity predicts subsequent personality change. Human Brain Mapping, 36(11), 4334-4345.

- Lehrer, P., et al. (2010). Heart Rate Variability Biofeedback: How and Why Does It Work? Frontiers in Psychology.
- Levenson, R. W. (1994). Human Emotion: A Functional View. In M. Lewis & J. Haviland (Eds.), Handbook of Emotions. The Guilford Press.
- Leventhall, G. (2007). What is Infrasound? Progress in Biophysics and Molecular Biology, 93(1-3), 130-137.
- Li, Q., et al. (2009). Forest Bathing Enhances Human Natural Killer Activity and Expression of Anti-Cancer Proteins. International Journal of Immunopathology and Pharmacology.
- Liebreich, J. (2002). A Historical Survey of the Influence of the Moon on Life on Earth. European Review.
- Lilly, S. (2019). Crystal Healing & The Chakra System. Independently published.
- Lipton, B. (2008). The Biology of Belief: Unleashing the Power of Consciousness, Matter & Miracles. Hay House.
- Llinás, R. R., & Pare, D. (1991). Of Dreaming and Wakefulness. Neuroscience.
- Lubart, R., Wollman, Y., Friedmann, H., Rochkind, S., & Laulicht, I. (2005). Effects of visible and near-infrared lasers on cell cultures. Journal of Photochemistry and Photobiology B: Biology, 80(2), 89-95.
- Lukianoff, G., & Haidt, J. (2018). The Coddling of the American Mind: How Good Intentions and Bad Ideas Are Setting Up a Generation for Failure. Penguin Press.
- Luskin, F., et al. (2002). A Review of Mindfulness-Based Stress Reduction for Children and Adolescents. Journal of the Society for Integrative Oncology.
- Lutz, A., Greischar, L. L., Rawlings, N. B., Ricard, M., & Davidson, R. J. (2004). Long-term meditators self-induce high-amplitude gamma synchrony during mental practice. Proceedings of the National Academy of Sciences, 101(46), 16369-16373.
- Maciocia, G. (2015). The Foundations of Chinese Medicine: A Comprehensive Text. Churchill Livingstone.
- Macmillan, S., et al. (2019). International Geomagnetic Reference Field: the 12th generation. Earth, Planets and Space.
- Mandea, M., & Korte, M. (2012). Geomagnetic jerks: Rapid core field variations and core dynamics. Space Science Reviews.
- Mannheim, K. (1928). The Problem of Generations. Kegan Paul, Trench, Trubner & Co.
- Mäntylä, E., et al. (2008). From Plant Traits to Plant Communities: A Multifunctional Approach to Predicting Plant Interactions in Natural Communities. Ecology Letters.
- Mate, G. (2003). When the Body Says No: Understanding the Stress-Disease Connection. John Wiley & Sons.

- Maus, S., et al. (2010). NOAA/NGDC candidate models for the 11th generation International Geomagnetic Reference Field and the concurrent release of the 6th generation Pomme magnetic model. Earth, Planets and Space.
- Mayer, F. S., Frantz, C. M., Bruehlman-Senecal, E., & Dolliver, K. (2009). Why is nature beneficial? The role of connectedness to nature. Environment and Behavior, 41(5), 607-643.
- McCarthy, B. (2010). The Intuitive Way: The Definitive Guide to Increasing Your Awareness. Jaico Publishing House.
- McCraty, R., et al. (2003). The Effects of Emotions on Short-Term Power Spectrum Analysis of Heart Rate Variability. American Journal of Cardiology.
- McGinn, B. (2006). The Essential Writings of Christian Mysticism. Modern Library.
- McNicholas, J., & Collis, G. M. (2000). Dogs as Catalysts for Social Interactions: Robustness of the Effect. British Journal of Psychology.
- McTaggart, L. (2002). The Field: The Quest for the Secret Force of the Universe. HarperCollins.
- McTaggart, L. (2007). The Intention Experiment: Using Your Thoughts to Change Your Life and the World. Simon and Schuster.
- Mills, P. J., et al. (2005). The Role of Biofields in Integrative Medicine. Alternative Therapies in Health and Medicine.
- Milton, D. J., et al. (1998). Infrasound from Atmospheric Sources: Characteristics of the Microbarom. Journal of the Atmospheric Sciences.
- Moltmann, Jürgen. *The Spirit of Life: A Universal Affirmation*. Fortress Press, 1992.
- Monroe, R. A. (1971). Journeys Out of the Body. Anchor Press.
- Nagel, T. (1974). What Is It Like to Be a Bat? Philosophical Review.
- Nagy, G. (1990). Pindar's Homer: The lyric possession of an epic past. Johns Hopkins University Press.
- Nelson, D. L., & Cox, M. M. (2005). Lehninger Principles of Biochemistry. W.H. Freeman.
- Niedermeyer, E., & da Silva, F. L. (2004). Electroencephalography: Basic Principles, Clinical Applications, and Related Fields. Lippincott Williams & Wilkins.
- Nielsen, A., Kligler, B., Koll, B. S., & Peacock, W. J. (2005). Acupuncture: An evidence-based review of the clinical literature. Annual Review of Medicine, 56, 49-63.
- Noddings, N. (2005). Philosophy of Education. Westview Press.
- Nutton, V. (2004). Ancient Medicine. Routledge.
- Odum, E. P. (1971). Fundamentals of Ecology. Cengage Learning.
- Orme-Johnson, D. W., et al. (2010). International Peace Project in the Middle East: The Effect of the Maharishi Technology of the Unified Field. Journal of Conflict Resolution.

- Oschman, J. L. (2000). Energy Medicine: The Scientific Basis. Churchill Livingstone.
- Palagini, L., et al. (2013). The Relationship Between Lunar Phases and Sleep Parameters: A Pilot Actigraphic Study in a Large Italian Sample. Sleep and Biological Rhythms.
- Perkins, J. (2001). Music as an Instrument of Diversity and Unity. Daedalus.
- Pinto, S. (2010). The Navajo concept of health. American Indian Culture and Research Journal, 34(2), 109-128.
- Plato. (2008). "The Republic." Penguin Classics.
- Polk, J. D. (1982). Schumann Resonances and Human Biologies. Journal of Biological Physics.
- Pollan, M. (2018). How to Change Your Mind: What the New Science of Psychedelics Teaches Us About Consciousness, Dying, Addiction, Depression, and Transcendence. Penguin Press.
- Popp, F. A., et al. (1988). Biophoton Emission: New Evidence for Coherence and DNA as Source. Cell Biophysics.
- Popp, F. A., et al. (1988). Electromagnetic Bioinformation. Urban & Schwarzenberg.
- Post, S. G. (2005). Altruism and Health: Perspectives from Empirical Research. Oxford University Press.
- Price, S. (1999). Aromatherapy for Health Professionals. Churchill Livingstone.
- Putnam, R. D. (2007). E Pluribus Unum: Diversity and Community in the Twenty-first Century. Scandinavian Political Studies.
- Quirke, S. (1992). Ancient Egyptian Religion. Dover Publications.
- Radin, D. (2006). Entangled minds: Extrasensory experiences in a quantum reality. Paraview Pocket Books.
- Radin, D. (2013). Supernormal: Science, yoga, and the evidence for extraordinary psychic abilities. Deepak Chopra Books.
- Rawls, J. (1971). A Theory of Justice. Belknap Press.
- Rinaldi, S., et al. (2020). The Scientific Foundation of Frequency Therapy in Clinical Practice. Journal of Integrative Medicine, 18(4), 265-277.
- Robertson, V. J., & Baker, K. G. (2001). A review of therapeutic ultrasound: effectiveness studies. Physical Therapy, 81(7), 1339-1350.
- Rocca, J. (2004). Galen on the brain: Anatomical knowledge and physiological speculation in the second century AD. Brill.
- Rosen, N. (2019). Vibrational Medicine: The #1 Handbook of Subtle-Energy Therapies. Inner Traditions.
- Rotton, J., & Kelly, I. W. (1985). Much Ado about the Full Moon: A Meta-Analysis of Lunar-Lunacy Research. Psychological Bulletin.
- Rubik, B. (2002). The Biofield Hypothesis: Its Biophysical Basis and Role in Medicine. Journal of Alternative and Complementary Medicine, 8(6), 703-717.

- Sagan, C. (1980). Cosmos. Random House.
- Salzberg, S. (1995). Loving-kindness: The Revolutionary Art of Happiness. Shambhala Publications.
- Saraswati, Swami Sivananda. *Kundalini Yoga: The Mysteries of the Fire*. The Divine Life Society, 2014
- Särkämö, T., et al. (2013). Music, Brain, and Rehabilitation: Emerging Therapeutic Applications and Potential Neural Mechanisms. In Music Perception.
- Särkämö, T., et al. (2016). Music Listening Enhances Cognitive Recovery and Mood after Stroke: A Randomized Controlled Trial. Journal of Music Therapy.
- Sartre, J.-P. (1943). Being and Nothingness. Philosophical Library.
- Satyananda Saraswati, S. (1984). Kundalini Tantra. Bihar School of Yoga.
- Schafer, R. M. (1977). The Soundscape: Our Sonic Environment and the Tuning of the World. Destiny Books.
- Scholem, G. (1949). Major Trends in Jewish Mysticism. Schocken Books.
- Searle, J. R. (1992). The Rediscovery of the Mind. MIT Press.
- Seligman, M. E. (2006). Learned Optimism: How to Change Your Mind and Your Life. Vintage Books.
- Senge, P. M., et al. (2008). The Necessary Revolution: How Individuals and Organizations Are Working Together to Create a Sustainable World. Broadway Business.
- Serpell, J. A. (2002). Companion Animals and Us: Exploring the Relationships between People and Pets. Cambridge University Press.
- Sharma, B. (2019). Kundalini Awakening: A Comprehensive Guide to Activating the Seven Chakras and Awakening the Kundalini Energy. Independently published.
- Sharma, Hari. (2015). Ayurveda: The Science of Self-Healing. Lotus Press.
- Sheldrake, R. (1981). A New Science of Life: The Hypothesis of Morphic Resonance. J.P. Tarcher.
- Siegel, D. J. (2010). The Mindful Therapist: A Clinician's Guide to Mindsight and Neural Integration. W. W. Norton & Company.
- Simmons, R. A. (2005). The Book of Stones: Who They Are & What They Teach. North Atlantic Books.
- Simmons, R. A., & Ahsian, N. (2007). The Book of Stones: Revised Edition. North Atlantic Books.
- Sirin, I. (1992). The Interpretation of Dreams. Islamic Book Service.
- Stein, D. K. (2003). Essential Reiki: A complete guide to an ancient healing art. Crossing Press.
- Stephens, M. (2010). Yoga Sequencing: Designing Transformative Yoga Classes. North Atlantic Books.
- Stevens, J. (2010). The secrets of Aikido. Shambhala Publications.

- Strogatz, S. H. (2003). Sync: The Emerging Science of Spontaneous Order. Hachette Books.
- Suzuki, D. T. (2010). Zen Buddhism: Selected writings of D.T. Suzuki. Anchor.
- Svoboda, Robert E. (1999). Prakriti: Your Ayurvedic Constitution. Lotus Press.
- Talbot, M. (1991). The Holographic Universe. HarperCollins.
- Tang, Y. Y., et al. (2015). The Neuroscience of Mindfulness Meditation. Nature Reviews Neuroscience.
- Tart, C. T. (1975). States of consciousness. E. P. Dutton.
- Taylor, J. (2001). Where People Fly and Water Runs Uphill: Using Dreams to Tap the Wisdom of the Unconscious. Warner Books.
- Tedlock, B. (1992). The Way of the Shaman: A Guide to Power and Healing. HarperOne.
- Teixeira, M. Z., et al. (2019). Full Moon Increases Sleep Latency. Current Biology.
- The Holy Bible: New International Version. Biblica, 2011.
- Thoma, M. V., La Marca, R., Brönnimann, R., Finkel, L., Ehlert, U., & Nater, U. M. (2017). The effect of music on the human stress response. PLoS ONE, 12(5), e0177805.
- Tiller, W. (1997). Science and Human Transformation: Subtle Energies, Intentionality and Consciousness. Pavior Publishing.
- Tisserand, R., & Young, R. (2014). Essential Oil Safety: A Guide for Health Care Professionals. Churchill Livingstone.
- Tolle, E. (1997). The Power of Now: A Guide to Spiritual Enlightenment. New World Library.
- Tononi, G. (2004). An information integration theory of consciousness. BMC neuroscience, 5(1), 42.
- Tononi, G., & Koch, C. (2008). The Neural Correlates of Consciousness: An Update. Annals of the New York Academy of Sciences.
- Toynbee, A. (1946). A Study of History. Oxford University Press.
- Translated by Swami Paramananda. (2019). *Upanishads.* Prakash Books.
- Trehub, S. (2001). Musical Predispositions in Infancy. Annals of the New York Academy of Sciences.
- Tyack, P. L. (2000). Functional Aspects of Cetacean Communication. In Cetacean Societies: Field Studies of Dolphins and Whales. University of Chicago Press.
- Ueshiba, M. (2019). The Art of Peace. Shambhala Publications.
- Ulrich, R. S. (1984). View through a Window May Influence Recovery from Surgery. Science.
- Van de Castle, R. L. (1994). Our Dreaming Mind. Ballantine Books.
- van der Kolk, B. (2014). The Body Keeps the Score: Brain, Mind, and Body in the Healing of Trauma. Viking.

- Van der Walt, L., & Burger, E. (2011). A Concept Analysis of Sacred Music as a Means to Promote Psychological Well-Being. Journal of Religion and Health.
- Various. (Date). *Buddhist Sutras*. Publisher.
- Vaughan, F. (1979). Awakening intuition. Anchor Press.
- Vickers, A. J., Cronin, A. M., Maschino, A. C., Lewith, G., MacPherson, H., Foster, N. E., ... & Acupuncture Trialists' Collaboration. (2012). Acupuncture for chronic pain: individual patient data meta-analysis. Archives of Internal Medicine, 172(19), 1444-1453.
- Vitale, J. E., & Viglione, D. J. (2015). More on Full Moons and Their Effect on Human Behavior. Journal of Psychosocial Nursing and Mental Health Services.
- Vogel, S. (2003). Comparative Biomechanics: Life's Physical World. Princeton University Press.
- Walsh, R., & Vaughan, F. (1993). Paths beyond ego: The transpersonal vision. TarcherPerigee.
- Wang, C., Bannuru, R., Ramel, J., Kupelnick, B., Scott, T., & Schmid, C. H. (2016). Tai Chi on psychological well-being: systematic review and meta-analysis. BMC Complementary and Alternative Medicine, 16(1), 1-16.
- Wang, X., Zhang, Y., Dong, Y., & Jiang, H. (2017). Effects of Gong Meditation on Stress, Anxiety, and Depression: A Randomised Controlled Trial. Evidence-Based Complementary and Alternative Medicine.
- Wang, W., & van Oudenhove, L. (2020). Therapeutic effects of sound meditation practice: A systematic review. Complementary Therapies in Medicine, 51, 102391.
- White, J. (2000). Kundalini, Evolution, and Enlightenment. Paragon House.
- Wiedemann, G. (2013). Tibetan Sound Healing: Seven Guided Practices to Clear Obstacles, Cultivate Positive Qualities, and Uncover Your Inherent Wisdom. Sounds True.
- Wilber, K. (1996). A Brief History of Everything. Shambhala Publications.
- Wilber, K. (2000). Integral Psychology: Consciousness, Spirit, Psychology, Therapy. Shambhala Publications.
- Wilber, K. (2007). Integral Spirituality: A Startling New Role for Religion in the Modern and Postmodern World. Shambhala.
- Wilson, E. O. (1984). Biophilia. Harvard University Press.
- Wiltschko, R., & Wiltschko, W. (2005). Magnetic Orientation in Animals. Springer.
- Woolger, R. J., & Woolger, J. (1988). The Goddess Within: A Guide to the Eternal Myths that Shape Women's Lives. Fawcett.
- Wu, Y. (2005). Chinese Symbolism and Art Motifs. Tuttle Publishing.
- Young, Hugh D., and Roger A. Freedman. University Physics. Addison-Wesley, 2012.

ACKNOWLEDGMENTS

I am deeply grateful to the following individuals whose wisdom, guidance, and support have illuminated my path on this profound journey of exploration and discovery:

- Preet Kaur: Kundalini Yoga and Sound Healer from Glastonbury, whose profound vibrational healing and deep insights have illuminated the path of meditation and chakra cleansing.

- Aaron & Alex for your unwavering support, and for being the beautiful souls your are.

- Tracey Bryan-Poole: Crystal Expert and Spiritual Healer, for her invaluable advice on crystal healing and her compassionate support on relationship recovery.

- Melody Cox: Aromatherapist, Life Coach, and Healer, whose wisdom and expertise in aromatherapy have brought clarity and balance to many lives.

- Swami Premananda: For sharing invaluable knowledge on Hinduism and philosophy, inspiring deeper exploration and understanding, and for your introduction into Ayurvedic traditions.

- FPMT Buddhism: The mind and its potential. Insights gained from this teaching program have been grounding and insightful.

- Georgie Fowle: Yoga Educator, for your knowledgeable guide whose expertise has contributed to understanding yoga for chakra flow.

Thank you to each of you for your unwavering support, wisdom, and inspiration. Your contributions have enriched this work immeasurably, and I am honoured to have had the opportunity to learn from each of you.

I also extend my sincere appreciation to the multitude of philosophers, scholars, sages, and seekers whose documented journeys of discovery have served as beacons of knowledge and inspiration, enriching the collective understanding of consciousness and its mysteries. There are too many too mention but the information is there if you seek it. I hope that by consolidating and referencing some of these people's thoughts, research and writing in the book it will guide you on your way.

With heartfelt appreciation,
    NJ Powell